MW00390383

Contents

author's note

Every time I revisit this manuscript in its preparation, I chuckle to myself about the grossly in-depth and tangled treatise I present to the reader with the aim of 'simplifying' the Peace process. It seems I use an awful lot of words to achieve a paradigm of simplicity.

And, to answer your question (yes, you asked a question by picking up this book), peace itself is easy – once you deconstruct your inherited and overly complicated perspective. It's getting through that process which takes some doing. You've spent a lifetime learning how not to do it (peace). It's gonna take a 'minute' to undo all of that ('unpeace'). It did for me (30 years once I started actively asking questions; let's hope you're a quicker study). So, in advance, thank you for your patience with the presentation of concepts, historical insights, scientific corollaries, and pontificating on my part.[1]

The assertions made in this book are based as much on intuition, deduction, and reason as they are in historical documentation and scientific discovery. *Facts are dead, intuition is alive.* Without the ability to synthesize and deduce, information on its own is of little consequence. Two people can look at the same painting and see different things. One, less experienced, sees a park with some people in it. While another, more experienced, sees a burdened mother with her two children; a deep, ongoing conversation of some weight between gentlemen; the joy of children playing; the fecund clouds on the horizon. Learned perspective can inform the lens through which we see.

Most of the historical and scientific supporting facts presented herein have been known for hundreds if not thousands of years. But the wrong lens has been applied to them. In this text I present these facts from an unconventional angle, along with the logic followed, for your consideration. This is a philosophical perspective piece based on historical research and scientific query, and founded upon deduction and intuition, in the light of the teachings of the ancient peace traditions. The pieces of this puzzle have been within our means for some time. Our lack of perspective has obscured the image. Until now that image has been blurred. In this manuscript it comes into focus. An image that illuminates and informs the observer of the bigger picture, the obscured connections between the pieces, and what they mean.

I wrote this book as the culmination of my deep desire for answers to existential truth. Having had a near-death, out-of-body experience in my youth after a grueling car accident of which I was the only survivor, I wanted an explanation for the state of ultimate Peace and the lack of mental and emotional processes that I experienced during the several minutes I was 'unshackled from the physical realm.'[2] For the absence of local identity and opinion, judgment and valuation as I had known them in the body. This book presents the 'knowing' I acquired after thirty years of seeking, of putting together the 'puzzle pieces' which had been laying around on the proverbial 'floor' for millennia. The truth I found was simultaneously simple, beautiful, and more empowering than I could have imagined. This process of discovery pointed me toward the Path of Peace. For which I am forever grateful.

With this said, I would like to bid you well on your path. I hope this practice serves you as it serves me. My benediction for you is, in the words of the Essenes, 'Peace be with you.' And as Jesus added, "...my peace I give to you."

with sincere gratitude,

preface
the title and the purpose

If you can't explain it simply,
you don't understand it well enough.
- Albert Einstein

The title of this book, 'Just Peace,' seems simple enough, but like its pursuit, can be more nuanced than it first appears. Our task here is to de-clutter the concept (easier said than done).

While peace is what most people hope to find through pleasant happenstance, good fortune, agreeable relationships, or perhaps moments of downtime away from the daily grind, true Peace is not a 'flickering flame' of external agents or luck. It is in fact the product of ongoing, intentional lifestyle choices, which we ourselves control.

Over thousands of years the founders of the ancient peace traditions observed and intuited mankind's Path of Peace (capitalized when referring to holistic peace, as opposed to lesser versions). These traditions converge and agree in profound ways on what it means to be human, how we can become aligned with the forces of nature for optimal health, and the simple means of experiencing true Peace in our otherwise complicated and - at times - stressful lives.

While peace is a worthwhile goal in and of itself, it also yields rewards beyond its own immediate function of calmness, serenity, and fulfillment. As scientists are beginning to more fully discover, peace in the body, emotions, and mind can significantly increase your lifespan while - and more importantly - simultaneously decreasing your end-of-life disease-span.[3]

The object of the title, 'Peace,' refers to the complete alignment and agreement of one's body, emotions, and mind with nature and natural law. This is the only means of experiencing pure, true, holistic, and total Peace. Partial peace, such as 'peace of mind' alone, falls short and does not serve one's overall health and personal evolution to its potential and ideal state.

The qualifier, 'Just,' implies several concurrent meanings, all of which apply. They are detailed here in the order that Merriam-Webster lists them. This prescription for Peace as taught by the Ancients (the founders of the ancient peace traditions) is:

- *reasonable*: it is based on reason, logic, natural science, and human experience dating back more than 12,000 years
- *proper*: that it considers all aspects of one's being, and as such conforms to a standard of correctness (or wholeness)
- *faithful to an original* (or prototype): this refers to its ancient and time-tested origins
- *in conformity with what is morally upright or good* (a.k.a righteous): it strives to uphold the highest ideals of humanity
- *deserved*: your body, mind, and spirit function at their utmost when in a state of peace. Regardless of your own perception of self-worth, your body, mind, and spirit need peace to operate at optimal levels.

- *legal*: there is certainly nothing illegal about the prescription for peace herein (currently; but laws change)
- *only*: meaning that it stands alone, without additional requirements or prerequisites. It alone is enough.

The method of Peace prescribed in this book comes with no strings attached. No gimmicks. No subscriptions. And no particular belief system, dogma, or doctrine is required to accomplish this, the most healthy and harmonious state of Being. True Peace is found from within, not from without. You and only you are responsible for creating Peace in your life. The only 'demons' you have to conquer are your own; the only 'guardian angels' you need are the natural and cosmic forces[4] which are already all around and within you: sun, air, water, earth, love, power, wisdom, and joy.

We, as intelligent beings with the ability to create imaginary paradigms; and further, having the tendency to reinforce those paradigms with others as to their 'realness' and validity, are really good at making things much more complicated than they have to be. I am speaking from personal experience. Just look at the first sentence of this paragraph. Guilty as charged. I think we like our overly complex ideas of life and living, of friend and foe, and of the spectrum of causes and effects of human politics, religion, and society. On some level they become entertaining for us, and our imaginations race with the fanciful stories we weave on their behalf.

When I first started putting this obscured information together, having been steeped in a Christian religious paradigm for decades, I felt like 'Truman,' the lead character of Andrew Niccol's 1998 film *The Truman Show*[5] (which ironically was released only five short years after my life-changing near-death experience). I started looking at the world and its constructs differently. I started to see how this misguided paradigm was reinforced systematically throughout society's institutions. Being 'enlightened' isn't all it's cracked up to be. You suddenly find yourself at odds with pretty much every societal norm. An outsider looking in. And the normalized complexities and priorities of the world lose value.

The Truth is much simpler than we seem to accept. In fact, it is as simple as a grain of wheat (Zarathustra), or as a mustard seed (Jesus), or as the lotus flower (the Buddha). When we realize, like Dorothy from *The Wizard of Oz*[6], that we had the 'ruby slippers' - the solution to our (man-made) problems - all along, life gets much simpler, less stressful, and more empowering. The Truth is simply - simplicity. As is made plain throughout this ancient method, simplicity in diet, in activity, in wants, in finances, in relationships, well... in fact everything, is the center stripe on the Path of Peace.

The purpose of this book is to present the common thread found throughout the ancient peace traditions, observed in various forms and practices (regardless of tribe, culture, religion, region, or heritage), which proved to be the most effective and efficient means of achieving holistic Peace. This thread exposes the connectedness and continuity of the peace traditions, both ancient and modern. The differences between them are superficial. Dig deeper and you will find their basic precepts and applications are fundamentally the same. Like the stark contrasts we see between groups of modern humans, originating in a few small clans thousands upon thousands of years ago; the wildly splintered spiritual traditions of today had austere beginnings as well.

We like to imagine that our ancient ancestors were more primitive, less intelligent, and less sophisticated than ourselves. We think we have evolved intellectually so far beyond our brutish ancestral heritage. But evidence points toward the contrary. Even if you discount many apparent indications of intellect and cunning in early man – like toolmaking (ca. 2.4 million years), controlled use of fire (ca. 1.7 million years), and weaponry (ca. 64 thousand years) – by 30,000 years ago 'modern' man had arrived.[7] If you passed by a *Homo sapien* of this era on the street today (albeit donning modern clothing and hairstyle), you'd likely not think anything unusual of the encounter at all.

When we look at early human manipulations, ingenuities, and structures; and their ability to overcome seemingly insurmountable obstacles (all without modern tools, heavy machinery, and computer technology), we often cannot fathom accomplishing these exceptional tasks even today. Notable structures such as Stonehenge, the great Egyptian pyramids, Myan cities, and Easter Island monoliths pale in age to sites such as Göbekli Tepe and Boncuklu Tarla (the latter of which is believed to be at least 12,000 years old). These last two (the most ancient of the listed sites), located in southern Turkey, are attributed with megalithic structures, food production techniques and the earliest controlled food systems, resident villages, an abundance of artifacts including tools and weapons, and the first cultural and religious structures.[8] These were accomplished by civilizations we tend to consider as comparatively 'primitive.'

And, from a different perspective, the indigenous tribes of the world (such as the Native Americans, of whom I proudly share heritage), who did not initiate the Industrial Revolution, but who maintained their simplistic harmonious lifestyle with nature and all living things, fostering their spiritual connection with these forces, were frequently referred to as 'savages.' This moniker from so-called 'civilized' societies which have pushed our world to the brink of disaster (and possibly extinction), for all their 'ingenuity.' I bewilder at the mentality one must have to think that concrete, microwaves, blue jeans, and cheeseburgers are advancing our evolution as beings on this planet when compared to the harmonious and intuitive ways of the indigenous peoples of the world. Who are the 'savages'? (Ironically posed, if that wasn't clear.)

Humans have arguably not become smarter over time. We might even be able to justify that the opposite is true, on average. Just over the past 100 years education standards in America have dropped significantly (as a career classroom teacher and college professor, I have firsthand experience of this trend). For all the information and 'college-readiness' with which we try to engorge High School students, the numbers enrolled in advanced placement courses now offered at American High Schools[9] rival the number of remedial courses students are taking once attending college[10] due to their substandard skill and knowledge base. Have you seen an 8th-grade graduation exam from the early 1900s?[11] Many advanced high schoolers or even college students today would struggle to pass this test.

The earliest hominids of our species, *Homo sapiens*, were as intelligent as modern humans, by all indications. And if that is correct, it is not likely that they (not actually the cryptic morons that popular media likes to sometimes imagine) by default credited the unseen forces of nature as being the product of 'magic' or mysticism. For one thing, we have just shown that they were as logical and grounded as the best of us. And for another, due to their position along the path of technological evolution, were too busy trying to survive, acquire food, and protect their people to be overly preoccupied with questions like 'where does the sun go at night?' (If you've ever been in a true survival situation, what did you spend your time thinking about?)

Were there mysteries? Certainly. But they knew where their nourishment came from, and what forces of nature were critical to maintaining their health and vitality; and for these things they were thankful. Intimately familiar with nature and the natural forces, they knew that there was a far greater intelligence and 'spirit' within nature than that of their own, and well beyond comprehension. They showed appreciation to (not 'of') the natural forces of sun, air, water, and earth for their life-giving sustenance. They acknowledged the true meaning of life through the cosmic forces of love, power, wisdom, and joy. They saw spirit ('God') in every phase of its ('his') Creation. And they taught their children to do the same, to show gratitude and reverence for the gifts of Nature, freely given to them by the creative Source of the universe. And their progeny continued this teaching over the generations.

This practice of veneration of the forces of nature and the cosmos is the essence of the ancient Peace traditions.

The Ancients handed down this knowledge from one generation and civilization to the next, to those among them who were 'empty vessels.'[12] Revealing the 'spirit of truth' – which has been the focus of many Faith movements throughout time immemorial – in its simplicity and innocence. Over time, man has taken the innocence of these teachings and made it complicated, cumbersome, and difficult; fraught with unnecessary motive, guilt, shame, ritual, and laws upon statutes upon decrees.

This prescribed system of the Ancients, in its purest form, is the focus of this book. This system of Peace works regardless of one's spiritual background or inclinations because it is founded entirely in natural phenomena. It is the historical basis of all faith and peace traditions. It is rooted in direct observation and subject to common experience. And modern science is starting to discover these truths, reinforcing the Ancients' observations and intuitions.[13] While these practices can result in a deep sense of spiritual awakening and awareness, due to their 'tapping' the faithful observer into higher states of consciousness, no claim of the other-worldly, of magic, or of miracles is made herein. Nor was any such claim made by the founders who practiced them[14] (though their followers may have made such associations out of a lack of understanding).

Consistently the progenitors of the various peace traditions regarded the natural forces of sun, air, water, and earth, and of the cosmic forces of love, wisdom, power, and joy as 'angels' or other such entities which assisted mankind in their personal evolution. There is a reason and a purpose for this personification of the forces of nature, which we will unravel later in this book. This concept of personification is a critical component in the process of personal evolution. Speaking allegorically to their followers, who were often not as sophisticated in their understanding, the Ancients presented this truth in ways that could be more easily comprehended, often being expressed in simpler, more conventional, or relatable terms.[15]

Jesus tells his followers, "I have yet many things to say to you, but you cannot bear them now. When the Spirit of truth comes, he will guide you into all the truth."[16] The wisdom and teachings Jesus *did* share with his closest followers were often expressed in parables, metaphors, and stories due to his followers' lack of readiness. Even then, they seldom fully understood the concepts he was imparting.

Muhammad is quoted in the Qur'an as saying "O you who believe! Ask not about things which, if made plain to you, may cause you trouble. But if you ask about them while the Quran is being revealed, they will be made plain to you."[17] That is to say that experience brings understanding, and that his followers had not yet attained the necessary experience – which unfolds in its proper time – to gain understanding.

The Buddha addresses discernment of the mysteries in the Kalama Sutta, wherein he is quoted as saying, "...don't go by reports, legends, traditions, scriptures, logical conjecture, inference, analogies, or agreement through pondering views. When you know for yourselves that certain qualities are skillful, blameless, and praised by the wise, and when these qualities lead to welfare and happiness, then you should adopt and follow them."[18] (Compare this to the Apostle Paul's teachings in Philippians.[19])

Here, the Buddha, Jesus, and Muhammad (and the Apostle Paul) agree. As is accredited to Zen Buddhism, "When the student is ready the teacher will appear..."[20] Or, in Jesus' words, "He who has ears, let him hear."[21]

If you are like the vast majority of people who have ever lived, in order to experience true holistic Peace you are going to have to metaphorically 'update your software' and 'reboot your hard drive.' Reinvent yourself. Experience the world from a fresh (though ancient) perspective. Empty your cup.

For the time it takes to read this book, try putting your paradigm on 'pause': what you think you know about peace, how to achieve it, who you are, what you are, what is real, what the rules are, what the truth is, what your purpose is, and what is ultimately important. Test the wisdom of the Ancients, comparing it to your own life and experience, and see if it lights a Path of Peace for you - if the precepts in this document find a resonance in your Being.

If no, you can always put your garb - your persona - of beliefs and identity back on and pick up where you left off. For those who find the teachings have meaning, I can personally testify to the profound impact on your personal life and health, the lives of those in your sphere, and your footprint on the planet.

And, at the very least, consider this simple recipe for a worthy life as taught by Zarathustra to his followers four thousand years ago, "Good thoughts. Good words. Good deeds."

– aspice, respice, prospice –

introduction
the ancient foundations of peace
and the modern dilemma

God communicates with us by way of all things.
They are messages of love.
-   Ernesto Cardenal

The ideas from which these practices are derived are
found in common across geographical regions,
cultures, and systems of belief, from before the
Neolithic Revolution[22] nearly 12,000 years ago (and
likely as far back as 40,000 years) in symbols for the
sun, moon, air, water, and other natural forces[23]; and
in hieroglyphs of the Sumerians eight-to-ten thousand
years ago.[24] Traces of these practices are found in the
teachings of ancient India, Tibet, China, Persia, Egypt,
Palestine, Greece, and many other cultures.[25] The
teachings appear in the Zend Avesta of Zarathustra[26],
Brahmanism[27], the Vedas[28], the Upanishads[29], the
Yoga systems of India[30], the teachings of the
Buddha[31], the Tibetan Wheel of Life[32], and the Law of
Moses.[33] More recent cultural practices following these
same precepts are found in the Pythagoreans and
Stoics in ancient Greece, the Adonic culture of the
Phoenicians, and the Alexandrian school of philosophy
in Egypt[34], to name a few.

The common thread across these traditions is that they
transcend place and time, finding voice from one
Enlightened to the next, bending to the sensibilities of
peoples and cultures, but always proving true. These
proven peace practices culminated in the most efficient

and effective system for peace and health in recorded history: that of the Essenes. The Essenes are the lesser-known sect of the Jews of Judea, along with their counterparts, the Pharisees and Sadducees, who are well-documented. Information about the Essenes was relatively sparse until the discovery in 1947 of the Dead Sea Scrolls, found in a vast network of caves near Qumran, containing hundreds of documents written, collected, and preserved by this inspired group of people.[35]

The teachings and ethics of the Essenes influenced later Roman Christian sentiments, leading to subsequent systems in Western culture.[36] The Essenes revered Enoch (the father of Methuselah in the Old Testament of the Christian Bible)[37] as their founder and Moses as their lawgiver. The Essenes served as the Hebrew *intelligentsia* and 'keepers of the Faith' under Moses[38], and gave us John the Baptist, John the Beloved, and Jesus, who was considered the great Essene Master. Even the epistles attributed to the Apostle Paul show indications of Essene influence.[39] Jesus presented the precepts of this Peace most elegantly in the seven Beatitudes of the Sermon on the Mount.[40]

First-century historians such as Flavius Josephus, Pliny the Elder[41], Philo of Alexandria, Tacitus, and others refer to the Essenes variably but consistently as "a race by themselves, more remarkable than any other in the world" due to their unique simple way of living, their unrivaled agricultural expertise, their unusually long life spans (living on average as much as four times the life expectancy of their contemporaries), their amazing strength and endurance late in life, and their being held in high regard by all who came into contact with them for their unfailing character and integrity. They were regimented, disciplined, pious, scholarly, generous, skillful agronomists and arborists, well-known in their time for their teaching and natural healing practices.[42]

The prescription for Peace as detailed here, as practiced by the Essenes, is based in nature and not supernature. They believed that Nature (capitalized to indicate nature on the cosmic scale as opposed to that of our planet alone) was the source of all wisdom and knowledge, so they paid great attention to how it behaved, what universal laws were found at its core, and what we humans could learn from these laws facilitating a more healthy and peaceful way of life.

The Essenes' healing practices were based on knowledge of natural herbal healing properties, the benefits of fasting, and the body's ability to heal itself given the right conditions of sun, air, water, and earth.[43] These were natural remedies (mostly preventative, like clean living, exercise, exposure to nature, a natural organic diet, and positivity, for instance) passed down from the Ancients before them.

It was the Essenes, valuing all ancient knowledge[44] (from prehistory to their own time and from every known culture), who perfected the system of Peace prescribed in this book. They lived by its precepts, to high regard as referenced by contemporary historians, for hundreds of years (if not thousands, dating back to their origins as a sect of Hebrews under Moses).

Our hectic, fast-paced society is not designed to cater to this prescription for Peace, so any degree of adherence requires an intentional effort and very likely a modification from that which the reader is accustomed. I know that it was (and continues to be) for myself a daily test of will due to the convenience and ready availability of unhealthy alternatives.

There is very little - if anything at all - that even vaguely resembles the idea of a simple, pure, and peaceful life in 'civilized' society today. Even in the time of Jesus (two thousand years ago) and back to the time of Moses (more than three thousand years ago), the Essenes separated themselves from the unhealthy tendencies of society. To achieve this separation, they established remote, self-sufficient farming communities in order to follow a pure, organic, unadulterated, and healthy lifestyle.[45]

The challenge of adapting this method of holistic Peace in our modern technological society is to be *in this world but not of this world*. Once starting down the path of modern sensibilities, sentiments, comforts, and - often unwittingly - abuses of nature and natural law, initiating a 'hard reset' is formidable and daunting at best.

But if we are to undo the slow death that modern society offers us, albeit packaged and marketed to be convenient, 'shiny,' and addictive, then individuals must become sober to the reality of mankind's dilemma. That of the adverse effect of our excessive, materialistic, technological, adversarial, unnatural lifestyle on our bodily and mental health, our relationships and sense of community, and the ecology of the planet. Our commitment to individual Peace, as atoms of a larger whole, may - on a planetary scale - be our only chance to reverse the damage we are doing to our home, Mother Earth.

These Peace practices, as collected from the teachings of the Ancients, have been annotated, combined with supporting historical research and scientific studies, and formed into an insightful and revealing guide toward the Path of Peace. As you begin to apply the concepts in this book, keep in mind that no one is perfect; that personal evolution is a 'muscle' which requires exercise; and that Peace is more about the journey than its destination.

We find humility and compassion through the experience of our own failings.

the nature of nature
mind or matter?

I have no special talent.
I am only passionately curious.
- Albert Einstein

If the teachings of the founders of the Peace traditions were based in nature and natural law, then there must be a natural logic found within them. While the teachings regarding 'Peace with the Body' and 'Peace with the Mind' are easily enough verified by scientific studies, 'Peace with the Spirit,' by definition, veers into the realm of philosophy. The premise that the Ancients maintained in their understanding of the Spirit is based on the observation of nature and natural law and by intuition (their ability to find patterns in nature and make informed deductions). From this they reasoned that what underlies all that exists is the Abstract: a formless field containing all forms and from which all forms derive. And that the phrase "as on earth, so in heaven" was true and literal, meaning that what applies in the material also applies in the immaterial.[46]

Given that logic, if the Source of all things is the Abstract (Spirit), then the essence of the material universe is one and the same with that of the immaterial universe. As some would put it, *the Creator breathes his Spirit into his Creation*. And if the Source of all things material and immaterial is the Abstract (Spirit; a.k.a. that which is formless yet which contains all forms), then Spirit is not supernatural, it is the essence of the natural world. Meaning it is as natural

1

as natural gets. The natural world is a product of the Abstract. Nature as we know it sprang from its womb. The progenitor of Nature cannot itself be supernatural, by definition.[47]

Fully understanding (or even believing that) this line of reasoning (is correct or not) is not a prerequisite to experiencing a successful state of Peace in your Being (capitalized to indicate all phases of your existence). It's kind of like churning milk into butter: you don't have to believe that it can, but if you use the right amounts of the right ingredients, follow the prescribed method, and just keep churning... *voilà*, butter (or at least cream, depending on when you give up).

The Peace practices of the Ancients were predicated on the subject experiencing an intimate relationship with the forces of nature and the cosmos.[48] (We will explain why in some detail in the upcoming pages.) This intimate relationship was prescribed through a series of 'Communions.' They are 'communions' and not 'meditations' precisely because the act of entering into communion with a person, place, or thing means to actively engage in relationship, to become open and vulnerable, and thus fully receptive to the energies of the object of communion. The act of meditation, on the other hand – when used in isolation and not as a means to achieving communion – is strictly a mental exercise wherein the subject passively concentrates on the object in question.[49] It is not intended to result in the subject becoming 'one' with the object. There is a psychological reason for the emphasis on 'communion' over 'meditation,' and a significant physiological

2

difference between the two approaches.[50, 51] And the Ancients knew it.

To prepare you for communion with concepts usually considered inanimate, non-personal, and utilitarian, we need to acquaint you with the perspective of the Ancients who taught these methods. We need to build a more personal connection between yourself and the forces of nature around you; between you and the source of creation; and between your mind, body, and spirit. To accomplish that task, it helps for you to understand the logic and reasoning behind the teachings of the Ancients.

The question of 'Mind or Matter?' is relevant in order for us to reconstruct the Ancients' approach to Peace. Is the source of all Creation material or immaterial? That is to say, does matter (the material) emerge from 'mind' (the immaterial), or is the 'illusion of mind' a product of material processes? This has been a point of contention among scientists (materialists) and philosophers since the time of Plato.[52] The issue with proving the negative in this case is that by definition the immaterial world - beyond the scope of scientific means - is just that. We cannot prove nor disprove the existence of the Spirit (immaterial) realm by scientific means. So, we depend on logical deductions, reasoning, anecdotal evidence, and philosophical estimations.

For the Ancients, there was no question. It was evident to them that all substance, both material and immaterial, was governed by an underlying force. Their acute awareness of the living processes in nature made the laws these processes followed obvious and

3

undeniable. Not only did they find the Law in all they observed, they felt a deep sense of connection to it. They fostered this connection to the benefit of their peace and health. The Essenes called this guiding force the 'One Law,' (Moses referred to it simply as 'The Law') because it was singular and immutable.[53] Other traditions refer to this same force variably as the 'Aether' (ancient Greeks), 'Brahman' (Hinduism), 'Dharma' (Buddhism), 'Asha' (Zoroastrianism), 'God' (Western religions), the 'Logos' (Stoics), the 'Tao' (various Chinese philosophies), 'Great Spirit' (certain indigenous tribes), 'Consciousness' (panpsychism), or the 'Vacuum' (the modern physics community), et al.

Scientists since before Einstein have hypothesized a single field in physics, which Einstein coined the 'Unified Field.' Over the course of time, science has successfully yielded the fields of electromagnetism (Maxwell 1865), quantum electrodynamics (Ampère 1827), and the Standard Model of quantum physics (many scientists during the latter half of the 20th c.).[54] None of these are complete pictures of what we observe in nature and the universe. The search for the Unified Field in theories such as Quantum Gravity, String Theory, Superstring Theory, M-Theory, Loop Quantum Gravity, and Supersymmetry, et al., is ongoing and inconclusive.[55]

The closest thing we have to a Unified Field theory is the 'marriage' of Einstein's 'General Relativity' and 'Quantum Mechanics,' developed by many scientists including Planck, Bohr, Schrödinger, Heisenberg, Born, Dirac, and others in the early 1900s.[56] Unfortunately, these marriage partners (General

4

Relativity and Quantum Mechanics) are currently separated, in counseling, and considering divorce on the grounds of 'irreconcilable differences.'

What quantum physics does tell us is that at the most fundamental level of matter, there is...

no   thing   there.[57]

That is to say, what we perceive as being concrete and physical is simply a massive coordination of the tiniest vibrations of energy. Little wiggling energetic fields. These fields, from the smallest quarks to the largest celestial formations, are self-organizing.[58] As a matter of fact, self-organization seems to be the primary preoccupation of the cosmos (i.e. crystallization, thermal convection of fluids, chemical oscillation, animal swarming, neural circuits, and black markets, to name a few).[59] So, these tiny wiggling energetic "no-things" organize themselves into larger particles, which organize themselves into even larger systems, which eventually become either intelligent, aware, self-preserving living entities or highly-organized, non-wasteful, recyclable 'inanimate' structures (which happen to complement each other symbiotically – an even higher order of self-organization).

It seems that what lies at the most fundamental level of existence might just be what the Ancients variably referred to as 'Mind,' meaning a conscious, intelligent willfulness. Or an intelligent, willful consciousness. Or a willful, conscious intelligence. Take your pick.

How can we substantiate assigning these attributes of consciousness, intelligence, and willfulness to the

Vacuum (the Source; that which is formless but which contains all forms)?[60]

We know that the Source is conscious because consciousness exists. A creation cannot contain anything that its creator does not possess within its potentiality. A tree cannot produce fruit for which it does not contain the 'intelligence' and the elements to produce. A creation contains the spirit of its creator. When you have an idea, your spirit imbues that idea. That idea is an expression of who and what you are. Your idea is not the totality of you, but it contains your essence. Your idea cannot be anything that you are not. Likewise, if we experience some degree of consciousness, and we find degrees of consciousness throughout Creation, then the Source must have the potentiality for consciousness. And if the Source has the potentiality for consciousness, it likely is conscious, per our observations of nature.

We know that the Source is intelligent because at the deepest levels of existence are plans, information, organization, designs, processes, and structure.[61] Every living entity has a body plan.[62] Science can trace the genes that orchestrate body plans from the most recent organism in the evolutionary timeline back to the earliest.[63] These genes can be transplanted between unrelated species and continue the work of constructing the body plan of the new host[64] (the same principle of adaptability applies to stem cells[65]). If this is the case, where is the body plan located? Is it materially based, or does it exist in the Abstract, in some immaterial 'archive'? These are questions science has yet to adequately resolve.[66] (Biochemist

6

and researcher Rupert Sheldrake has coined the phrase 'Morphic Resonance' to this immaterial source of body plans and the instinctual heredities within like systems[67], to mixed reviews.) And this doesn't begin to address instinctual behaviors post-birth.

If the answer is that biological body plans are derived from the immaterial, science will never be able to answer that question by empirical evidence. Because there will be none. The Abstract, or 'Spirit' realm, is beyond scientific means. And just because a thing cannot be proven scientifically does not mean it does not exist. (You can't scientifically prove that I love my wife and children, but I assure you that I most certainly do.) It just means it is beyond our material 'grasp.'

We know that the Source is willful because there is desire in Nature. Nature acts with intent. It has motivation and purpose. That purpose can be deduced from simple observation. The most fundamental purpose of nature is survival - to continue into the future by any means necessary - and by extension procreation or replication, which are functions of the former. The lifeforce, when viewed as a single force of nature, and not in its many manifestations, does not show favoritism or preference for any one mode of life (not even us). It simply asks the questions, "What is possible?' and "What is the most efficient and effective adaptation?" It explores every possibility, embracing that which works, and discarding that which does not.[68]

In nature, there are no answers, there are only questions. What appear to be answers are themselves further questions. In this continuum of the lifeforce, it seems its sole purpose is to persist. Eternally. The Source's goal is Eternal Life. And all the processes of the Living Force converge toward that end. The compulsion to live is the primary expression of will.

From the Source's relentless questions emerged the material universe and eventually biological life. From these questions emerged inevitable Man – self-aware, intelligent, and capable of deviation from Nature.[69] Man's intelligence is also capable of communion with the One Law, the Source (which we have established is theoretically conscious, intelligent, and willful[70]).

Our intelligence (or Thinking Body) can commune with the Abstract because our consciousness is one and the same in essence (substance) as that of the Abstract (Spirit, the One Law). According to the Ancients, upon death our 'consciousness' continues. Our perceived *local consciousness* never completely vacated the *cosmic stream of consciousness* upon our birth, and it doesn't cease after our physical death. Your consciousness is consubstantial with the One Law which existed before the material universe and will continue after the universe ceases to physically exist.

> **The Soap Bubble Analogy:** Like a soap bubble popping, the integrity of the soap membrane fails, but the air inside was air before the bubble existed, remained air while encased in the bubble, and is reabsorbed into the air from which it came once the bubble expires. (Remember this analogy, it comes up a few more times.)

We get way deep into this subject in the next section of the book, 'the holy trinity of self.'

It has been said that mankind strives to thrive, not just survive. It is in his DNA. The desire to continue expansion and dominion of all that he surveys. But instead of turning inward, toward his spirit, seeking to commune with the Creator through the elevation of his personal evolution, mankind has turned outward toward the material world to satisfy his desire for expansion and dominance. But this outward thriving, which is confused for progress, is the source of man's demise. True wisdom, peace, love, progress, and expansion is found within, beyond the physical to the spiritual center of one's being.

To thrive in the material is the path of Death. To thrive in the immaterial is the path of Life. This was the message of all the great masters of Peace.

the holy trinity of self
and why holistic peace is so important

> ...we cannot doubt of our existence while we doubt.
> - René Descartes

The title of this section, 'the holy trinity of self,' contains three key factors, each of which could inspire its own chapter. But for our purposes, we will try to keep the concepts as concise and uncluttered as possible.

S E L F

Let's start with the object of the phrase, 'Self' (with a capital 'S' because we are talking about the entirety of your Being, all phases of your existence). Your 'Self' in this context refers to the aggregate of your physical self (Acting Body), your emotional self (Feeling Body), and your mental self (Thinking Body), which are bound and unified by an all-encompassing Spirit Self. Think of your Spirit Body encasing your Acting, Feeling, and Thinking Bodies in the way an atom contains its electrons, protons, and neutrons, uniting them into one coherent entity (see the graphic representation of 'Self/Being' below; this parallel is a profound correlate).

The Ancients taught that your Spirit Self (the Ancients also refer to this as your 'Higher Self') is the archetype of your most perfect potentiality – physically, emotionally, and mentally. Think of it as the blueprint of the ideal you. It exists in the Abstract (that which is formless yet which contains all forms) and 'speaks' to your 'Lower Self' (the aggregate of your material

10

experience through body, emotions, and mind; the Higher Self has a counterpart in the Lower Self which is known as the 'Inner Critic[71].' It speaks to you, too. But it's typically more negative. Avoid listening to that guy. He's usually bad news.). The easiest way to think of these two aspects of your Being is that the Higher Self resides primarily within the immaterial realm (Spirit, Abstract) and your Lower Self resides primarily in the material realm (physical, emotional, and mental).

Your Body is materially bound. Your Spirit is immaterially bound. The link between them is the Mind, which dwells in both the material and the immaterial. The Mind can interact with both the Body and the Spirit, through thoughts, which can regulate your material being (emotions and actions) to some degree but which also transcend the physical to commune with the immaterial because they share the same essence (think of the soap bubble). The Body cannot directly interact with the Spirit, nor the Spirit the Body, except through the Mind. The health of the Body supplies the health of the Mind. And the health of the Mind supports the health of both the Body and the Spirit. The health of the Spirit is a natural result of the health of both the Body and the Mind. In this way the phases of your existence are entangled, at least while a part of you resides within the material universe.

The Body is subject to material laws. It knows only that which is material. The Mind, which crosses the material and immaterial boundary, knows emotions and thoughts. Emotions are of the 'material realm exclusively, based on chemical reactions within the Body. However, the Mind directs the emotions by its thoughts, both conscious and unconscious; the unconscious rooted in our evolutionary mechanism, and the conscious tied to the formless Source which contains all forms. This part of our Mind touches (or interacts with) our Spirit, which is fully a part of the Abstract (or immaterial).

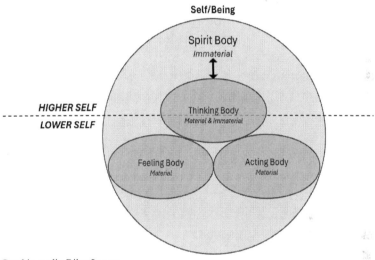

Graphic credit: Riley Larson

The Spirit experiences neither thought nor emotion[72] because these are the result of physical processes. It is difficult for us to imagine that the Spirit Body is distinct from our Thinking and Feeling Bodies. We can't imagine not having thoughts, as we struggle to accept the idea of ourselves being without emotion. But this is only because our experience is rooted primarily in the physical for much of our lives, and for some - less evolved - its entirety.

12

Once your Self transcends the physical, usually via death, and is truly freed of its biological 'membrane' (again, recall the soap bubble), there is no use for thoughts or emotions as we experience them materially. You become one with the Cosmic Ocean of Thought - the Mind of God - outside of time and space, which contains all Knowledge, Wisdom, Love, Power, and Joy.

Thoughts and emotions as physical processes require the passing of time and a location in space. So, once the Spirit is released from the Body, in the place of thought you now *become* Knowing-Wisdom (ultimate understanding). Instead of emotion you *are now* Love-Power-Joy (complete acceptance). You no longer experience these things as temporal parts of your Being, you *embody* them. You, having become one with the Source of all things material and immaterial, are consubstantial with all of Creation. This freedom, or eternal Peace, is in fact free also from your former material-based opinions, cares, values, judgements, or affiliations (these things do not facilitate Peace.) You are simply Awareness.[73]

Conscious, Intelligent Awareness.

This union with the All Father, yielding eternal Peace, has been referred to over the millennia in several ways: 'Heaven' by Christians, 'Aether' by the ancient Greeks, 'Nirvana' by Buddhists, 'Asha' by Zoroastrians, and so on. This ascension to Universal or Cosmic Consciousness - also referred to as Christ Consciousness[74] - can be (and is popularly believed to have been) experienced premortem by certain individuals - and not so coincidentally, some of the

13

founders of the Ancient Peace traditions - masters such as Enoch, Zarathustra, Moses, Elija, the Buddha, Pythagoras[75], and (arguably) Jesus.[76]

For those wondering how to achieve this monumental task premortem...

Proper alignment of your Lower Self with nature and natural laws facilitates access to higher states of consciousness. Your Higher Self is drawn to communion with the All Father. It constantly attempts to influence the Lower Self toward a state of harmony with the forces of Nature and the Cosmos. If this occurs, it results in the Higher and Lower Selves aligning into a seamless unity. To do so would require the perfection of the body, emotions, and mind to match the archetype of your Higher Self, which exists in the Abstract (every time you see the word 'Abstract' in this document, associate it with the phrase "that which is formless yet which contains all forms").

According to the Ancients, the purpose of perfecting your body, emotions, and mind to align with your Higher Self is to fulfill the perfection of your Spirit Self, facilitating full and unobstructed communion with the Source, the Creator, the One Law, the All Father, the Heavenly Father, or, as some refer to him, God. These are culturally-specific terms representing the same concept - the creative source of all substance, both material and immaterial.

The 'Abstract' that I keep mentioning does not refer to something which is theoretical. It is defined as the immaterial expression of a quality which is separate from an object. That it exists as an ideal in the Spirit

14

(non-physical) realm with a correlate in the physical realm. If you do not follow this reasoning, a cruder and less effective way to express the concept of 'Higher Self' is 'your best self' (a phrase I use with my kids frequently when discussing poor choices; usually mine, not theirs). But, for psychological reasons, personifying these concepts makes the connection to them stronger and decidedly more effective. The concept of personification is discussed in more detail in the next section of this book.

The Spirit - which resides in the Abstract - contains within it the perfect archetype of your physical being, emotional being, and mental being. This is what we call your 'Higher Self.' Connecting with your Higher Self means accessing the purest potential of your Being, and adapting your body, emotions, and mind to more resemble this archetype. The choices you make with regard to the healthful maintenance of your physical self (diet, exercise, exposure to nature), the moderation you maintain in your emotional self (love, joy, peace), and the fostering of the highest thoughts possible in your thinking self (positivity, curiosity, creativity) bring you closer to perfect Peace (health; life) or further from it (disease; death).

Our charge, as stewards of these phases of our existence, is to strive to perfect all three toward their ideal form, which exists within the Abstract of our Spirit Body. The achievement of the perfect alignment of our material body (Lower Self) with its ideal form in the Abstract (Higher Self), facilitates perfect union of our Acting, Feeling, and Thinking Bodies into one fully realized Being, which I am referring to here allegorically as 'the holy trinity of self.'

It is at this point, the perfection of your Being (your Spirit Self), that you become one with the Source, the One Law. This is what the Ancients referred to variably as 'Cosmic Consciousness' or 'Christ Consciousness.' Creating perfection in the physical, emotional, and intellectual parts of ourselves is like the locking mechanism of a padlock, which, when aligned properly, releases the shackle of the physical realm to allow the Spirit to experience complete freedom - ultimate Peace.

H O L Y

The qualifier "holy" in this phrase 'the holy trinity of self' expresses a degree of sacredness, of having a divine quality. At the root of many, if not all, of our self-inflicted health issues is tied - no, bound - to how we perceive ourselves. The Ancients taught that your body, emotions, and mind are gifts from the Creator, the Source. They are of 'divine' origin and essence. And for that reason alone, are - by definition - holy.

The problem is that we do not treat ourselves with any degree of 'holiness.' We do not venerate our body (and by extension emotions and mind) as sacred. We treat it as if it were disposable, relatively insignificant, and simply a 'sack of flesh' which does our bidding. That is, we take our body for granted until we can't any longer, due to failed health or acute pain. Then we might at long last start to appreciate it for what it is and the peace it should be experiencing; if it weren't for our own selfish, short-sighted, immature, uninformed, and/or excessive behaviors.

In the Christian Bible, the Apostle Paul is quoted as saying, "Or do you not know that your body is a temple of the Holy Spirit, who is in you, whom you have received from God?"[77] This concept is reflected in Buddhism as one's true 'being' existing within and without the physical.[78] In this way, the body, which we experience directly, is the conduit through which we access our Higher Self. Taoism regards nature as the ultimate experience[79], similar to the Essenes' naturalistic view. In this way, the body is to be venerated in its natural form as the source of all wisdom, both material and immaterial. In Islam, the body is the vessel of spiritual experience and must be purified.[80] It is the physical representation of the state of one's spirit. In Hinduism, the phases of one's Being, beginning with the body, facilitate ascension to Brahman.[81] In this way it is to be held as sacred, as a temple.

If the body is a temple, then it is - again, by definition - holy. Or at least it should be treated as if it were holy, sacred, venerated. When you begin to treat your body as holy, you become mindful of the quantity and quality of the substances you put into it; the quantity and the quality of sun, air, water, and earth to which it is exposed; how much movement and exercise it gets; the thoughts in your mind, which mitigate the emotions, which can wreak havoc on the body[82] if not kept in check; among many other physical concerns. The emotions and mind reside in, interact with, and are subject to the body.

And if all things material and immaterial derive from the Source of all Creation - which is formless, but which contains all forms - then the body, emotions, and mind are of its essence. Everything that you are is consubstantial with the creative force of the Universe. And if the Source of the universe is somehow holy, sacred, and to be venerated, then so is everything that constitutes you. The body, emotions, and mind are to be held to the degree of sacredness to which the creative force of life is due.

And even if you do not follow this reasoning, you would do well to treat your body as if it were sacred. The health benefits you experience in your body will correct a thousand 'sins' you have committed toward it in your past. The self-healing power of the body, aided by the forces of nature and the cosmos, is sufficient to correct many, if not most, if not all of the otherwise avoidable physical health issues you do now or ever will face. And, like the Essenes of two thousand years ago, the regimented practice of proper diet, fasting, regular exposure to nature, conveying sincerity to others, expressing love and compassion to all, and experiencing gratitude and joy in your daily life heals the body, mind, and soul.

TRINITY

The subject in the title of this chapter, 'trinity,' has already largely been covered in the discussion of the other two terms, 'self' and 'holy.' The "trinity" we are talking about refers to the three parts of your Being - distinct but inextricably linked - body, emotions, and mind. We call these your Acting Body (physical), your Feeling Body (emotional), and your Thinking Body (mental).

And to give you cause for pause…

The Ancients taught that you are not simply a receiver of energies, you are a transmitter.[83] Yes, you are akin to a two-way radio. You are subject to the planetary Oceans of Thought and Feeling (which are the aggregates of all the thoughts and emotions of all earthbound beings), but you also contribute to them, radiating your thoughts and feelings to every living terrestrial being in real-time. This is the equivalent of 'blessing' or 'cursing' others by simply holding positive or negative thoughts and feelings within your Self, because you radiate the energies created by your thoughts and feelings, which affect others.

If you feel there is too much hate in the world, stop hating. If you feel there is not enough patience in the world, be more patient. And on and on. The saying, "Be the change you want to see in the world"[84] (paraphrase credited to Mahatma Gandhi), could not be any truer.

In Summary…

The Ancients taught that the Thinking (mental) Body exists in both the Spirit (immaterial) realm and the physical (material) realm simultaneously. For this reason, the Thinking Body can regulate both the Feeling (emotional) Body and the Acting (physical) Body to a limited degree, but it can also commune with the Spirit realm (the Abstract; that which is formless, yet which contains all forms) because they both reside in the immaterial (the Spirit Body completely, the

Thinking Body partially). The Feeling Body resides in and is subject to both the Thinking Body and the Acting Body. It can be controlled to some degree by one's thoughts, but only partially, as it is also subject to the physical body.

The health of one phase of Self affects the health of the others. Disease radiates from one to the others. The health of the body affects the emotions, which in turn affects the mind, and interchangeably from any one phase to the others. The three phases of your Being are intertwined until physical death, at which point your Spirit Body - your Consciousness - is released from its mortal 'anchor' and is reabsorbed (or attempts to reabsorb) into the Abstract (Spirit realm; Cosmic Consciousness; recall the Soap Bubble analogy).

Buddhist traditions suggest that if your Being is not purified to unite with the Source/One Law/God at the time of death, you cannot achieve 'Nirvana' (end the cycle of rebirth and death) and are thus rejected back to the mortal form to continue your personal evolution (this is referred to as 'reincarnation'). This concept would agree with how natural systems behave with regard to the absorption or rejection of foreign or impure entities, which we discuss in the next section, entitled 'the concept of communion.'[85]

Now that you've been introduced to the Ancients' teachings on Self, we can 'level up' and discuss how your Self is utilized in the act of communion, resulting in the attainment of optimal Peace, as taught by the Ancients. This we will do in the next section, labeled 'the concept of communion.'

the concept of communion
an old way of thinking in a new landscape
(or old tricks for new dogs)

> The successful warrior is the average man,
> with laser-like focus.
>
> -   Bruce Lee

The Ancients referred to the Source of all things material and immaterial variably as the 'All Father,' the 'One Law.' They showed gratefulness to their Earthly Mother (a.k.a. Gaia, Mother Earth, Mother Nature, etc.), from whom their body was formed. They revered the forces of nature and the cosmos as 'angels' assisting them on their path of personal evolution.

The founders of the ancient peace practices did not consider these personifications as literal[86], as if the forces of Nature were independent sentient beings which resided in the heavens and could appear and disappear at will, showing up to chasten or protect a person in time of need. They did not 'worship' the forces of the Earth and the Cosmos as deities. They knew that the forces of Nature do not require our worship, nor our prayers, nor our devotion; but that *the experience of intimacy, relationship, trust, and love fully exposes one's whole Being for healing and renewal.* For this reason it was necessary to foster a spirit of communion with these forces, not for the object of the communion, but for its subject. Us.

The application of these concepts to the Ancients was with the purpose of yielding the highest degree of effectiveness in the human biological mechanism, based on their knowledge of human psychology and physiology. These personifications create a sense of 'communion' with the forces of nature and the cosmos, enhancing and extending our own conscious awareness of self, purity, and perfection.

The initial step on the Path of Peace is to enter into a state of communion, which offers the highest degree of intimacy. To achieve this, one must see themselves as intricately and inseparably linked to all things material and immaterial around them, that these things are one with the Living Force and can be communed with, and that there is a standard of perfection to strive for in one's personal evolution.

This standard of perfection was what the Ancients referred to as one's 'Higher Self.' Within each of us is an ideal state of being with regard to physical health, compassion and love, acts of kindness, positivity and high-mindedness, right choices, fairness and objectivity, and much more. This Higher Self gently whispers to us, informing our decisions and guiding us toward the right and true. If we are wise, we listen. But there are many conflicting motivations in our psyche and many outside influences which can cause deviation from what we know to be right. And if we muffle the voice of our Higher Self long enough, we can mute it entirely.

How can we know that there is a Higher Self within our consciousness?

You are your body,
but you can observe your body
from an outside perspective.

You are your emotions,
but you can observe your emotions
from an outside perspective.

You are your thoughts,
but you can observe your thoughts
from an outside perspective.

This means that your Higher Self exists outside of your body, emotions, and thoughts. The Ancients taught that this Higher Self, which exists in the Abstract (the Spirit realm; that which is formless yet which contains all forms) has the capacity to commune with the highest forces in the Universe and can itself commune with the One Law, the All Father, the Source of all that is material and immaterial.

In order for your material (physical) self to experience oneness with the One Law, it must be purified and perfected, because the One Law is pure and perfect by definition. An impure substance cannot be received into a pure living system without being rejected. (For instance, your own body will - ideally - amass forces to defend itself from something that enters your organism which seems not to belong or which otherwise compromises the system.[87]) The means of perfecting your Acting Body (physical body), your Feeling Body (your emotions), and your Thinking Body (your thoughts) is ascendance through communion to higher states of consciousness, which is what the Ancients referred to as the process of personal evolution.

The ultimate goal of holistic Peace is for you to create resonance with your Higher Self, which exists in the Abstract. (Creating resonance with your Higher Self is the purpose of the next three sections of this book, 'peace with the body,' 'weekly self-inventory,' and 'communions and contemplations.') This occurs when your body, emotions, and mind are in harmony with the forces of nature and the cosmos. Attaining this highest state of consciousness, the experience of Higher Self, facilitates communion with the One Law, the All Father, in the most direct and intimate way. Sustaining this connection to the All Father is referred to as ultimate Peace.

The most well-documented use of the concept of the Abstract in the teachings of the Ancients comes from the New Testament of the Christian Bible. The most frequent subject which Jesus is documented as discussing in the Gospels is "the kingdom of heaven," or variably, "the kingdom of God" (which are interchangeable).[88] Jesus' use of these equivalent phrases is a direct reference to the Abstract which the Ancients taught their followers to use as a measure of their personal evolution.

In Jesus' "kingdom of heaven" (the Abstract; or Spirit realm), everything exists in its most perfect and optimal state. In this reference, "heaven" or "God" is the One Law, formless yet containing all forms. It is the aggregate of the highest ideals of body, emotion, and intellect. When Jesus proclaims the "kingdom of heaven," "...on Earth as it is in heaven," or any other "heaven" reference, he means that the power to experience perfection in our Being (body, emotions, and intellect) is within our means. He is calling on all of us to strive for perfection and purity in our Lower Self to match that of our Higher Self, which exists in the Abstract (a.k.a. the fabric of Creation, the Mind of God, 'heaven').

Jesus taught his followers to pray following a certain model. In this model prayer, Jesus refers to the above concepts. Commonly known as the 'Lord's Prayer,' it served to frame his follower's perspective in a way that would orient their Being toward the Path of Peace. Below are both the literal prayer[89] (exoteric form) and its conceptual interpretation (esoteric form), according to the precepts as taught by the Ancients.

Original text
Our Father in heaven,
hallowed be your name.
Your kingdom come.
Your will be done,
on earth as it is in heaven.
Give us this day our daily bread,
And forgive us our debts,
as we have also forgiven our debtors.
And do not bring us to the time of trial,
but rescue us from the evil one.

Conceptual Interpretation
The All Father/One Law/Source which is in the Abstract (Spirit), I place myself in reverence to you and hold you sacred. I will strive for purity and perfection in my body, emotions, and mind to create oneness with my Spirit and to reflect the

25

perfection and purity of my Higher Self in my Lower Self. I am grateful for the bounty you provide through the Earthly Mother; and I know that the experience of peace in my own body, emotions, and mind is realized through my right actions and treatment of others. I will avoid the temptations of this world and silence my own inner urges toward destructive thoughts, words, and deeds.

In this prayer, Jesus taught his followers to bring themselves into a state of humility, openness, and vulnerability; to be reminded of their responsibility for the health and peace of their body, emotions, and mind through communion with the forces of nature and the cosmos and for the ongoing process of perfecting these phases of their experience; to maintain a state of gratitude to the earth for its nourishment, the elements of which the body is formed; that the health and peace of their Being is affected by the manner in which they treat others; and that they must be mindful of their carnal nature and of avoiding situations which may cause them to deviate from the Path of Peace.

Whether you believe literally these concepts as taught by the Ancients or not, putting yourself into a state of intimate relationship with the creative force of nature opens you up as a receiver for energies that exist within and around you, improving your health, extending your life, and bringing you joy and peace. The point of the task is not to necessarily 'believe' that the forces of nature are living beings and that you can have a relationship with them. The point is to open yourself to a state of vulnerability, wherein your entire Being becomes receptive to these energies. The same forces of nature from which you are derived and by which your health and vitality are sustained.

Optimizing your ability to receive these energies, they can work at their most efficient and effective levels, empowering your self-healing processes to be maximized, your vital functions to be strengthened, and your sense of peace and joy to be naturally reinforced through the chemical processes of your body.

It cannot be overstated, the qualitative difference between the act of 'communion' and simple 'meditation.' Meditation must be the initial act of the communion experience, as the mind brings the rest of our Being into a state of relationship with the object of communion, allowing our body and emotions to become open and receptive. Meditation facilitates communion, which is the target state of consciousness. The act of communing puts one into a degree of intimate relationship, a state of vulnerability and openness, allowing the forces of nature to penetrate deeply into the physical, emotional, and mental bodies of the subject. Meditating is typically viewed as primarily a mental exercise, wherein the subject is separate from the object of meditation. The effectiveness of the act of meditation alone is insignificant when compared to the profound absorption of energies which a state of communion facilitates.

As an example, people who claim to have had a 'religious experience' have put themselves (their complete Being) into the highest possible degree of openness and vulnerability prior to the experience, facilitating communion with their Higher/Spirit Self. Before having this experience, their mind was fully open to - even welcoming expectantly - the object of communion, their heart was full of love and devotion to it, and their thoughts, emotions, and body were receptive to its energies. When these things align, connection happens and the result is tangible (experiential) to the subject.

What science and medicine are discovering in case studies and under microscopes (and of which mankind has been aware for thousands of years through experience) is that one's body, emotions, and mind function at their utmost when in a state of peace.[90] Many of us don't feel deserving of peace because the ways we have thought, spoken, and acted in the past have been at times deplorable, hurtful, petty, and selfish. But, regardless of how ill your thoughts, words, and deeds have been leading up to this point in your life; your body, emotions, and mind - as unwitting minions of your intention - deserve peace. If you think of yourself as being the custodian of the body, mind, and spirit to which you have been 'assigned,' then your charge is to maintain and continuously improve them as their steward, to afford them as much peace as is possible so that they can perform at their most optimal state.

In popular psychology today, many tend to think of peace as being isolated to our thoughts or state of mind. We even have a phrase for it: "peace of mind." And while Peace with the Mind is a contributor, it alone does not facilitate holistic Peace. Holistic Peace

28

includes 'Peace with the Body,' 'Peace with the Emotions,' and 'Peace with the Mind.' As humans, we are all three of these things. So, peace in one area does not constitute Peace on the whole. If you have peace of mind but not of the body or emotions, you are still not at peace, not really.[91]

We also tend to think of 'peace of mind' as meaning that we are content to accept our situation (including dis-ease in our body, feelings, and/or thoughts), and that this 'coming to terms' with our situation by its own accord can bring us peace. According to the Ancients, this may serve as a placebo but it does not place us in a state of true Peace. I would go so far as to say that the Ancients would not consider a person who suffers with illness or inharmony in their body, and/or emotions, and/or thoughts to be 'at peace' in any true sense.

While being content with one's less-than-ideal condition may bring a degree of mental ease (some might call it numbness), it is the daily pursuit of health and vitality in all three aspects of our human existence which brings holistic Peace. To the Ancients, Peace meant health and proper alignment of one's physical, emotional, and mental phases with Nature and natural laws. Regardless of your degree of contentment with your life-situation, if you are not routinely exposing yourself to nature, practicing healthy eating habits, getting sufficient exercise, are abusing the environment, abusing others, and allowing negativity to reside in your mind (and subsequently your body and emotions), for instance, then you can never experience true Peace. At least according to the Ancients and their teachings. And I agree.

In that spirit, the 'communions and contemplations' featured in this book serve to point the observer toward 'Peace with the Mind' and 'Peace with the Emotions,' but there are certain prescriptions of lifestyle which the Ancients practiced in addition to these Communions which facilitated 'Peace with the Body.' We present them prior to the section on 'communions and contemplations' because Peace with the Body is paramount to the other two phases of your experience. Aligning your physical body with Nature and natural laws always takes precedence, according to the teachings of the Ancients.

The teachings of the Quran detail a holistic approach to peace, beginning with physical health, then addressing emotions and thoughts as a means to experiencing spiritual health and facilitating oneness of Being with God.[92] The term 'Islam' itself derives from the Arab word for 'peace,' *salaam*.

Taoism emphasizes the interconnectedness of body, mind, and spirit for optimal health; explicitly focusing on the body's innate natural ability to heal itself, given right ways of living.[93]

Jesus is associated with several separate documented healings[94] throughout the New Testament of the Christian Bible. His overwhelming focus is on the subject's physical health in every instance. He is only documented as twice giving what might be interpreted as follow-up moral instruction with someone "made well" in his presence (if you don't count telling them to

30

make offerings at the temple): (1) in John 5:14 to the blind beggar at Beth-zatha, "Do not sin any more, so that nothing worse happens to you"[95]; and (2) in Luke 8:43-46, "Go in peace," to the woman suffering from hemorrhages; meaning 'be well'. Neither of these is overtly 'judgy,' and he uses very few words to make his point. Some might even consider these as simply benedictions, like telling someone to 'have a nice day.' In all noted instances, Jesus himself proclaims that his healing encounters were 'faith healings,' in which one's own faith "made them well." [96]

The practices in the next section, labeled 'Peace with the Body,' are ideals which the Ancients practiced and taught to their followers. They are prescribed to align one's physical being with Nature and natural law, further facilitating the larger goal of personal evolution.

peace with the body
a lifestyle supplement

An authentic life is the most personal form of worship.
Everyday life has become my prayer.
- Sarah Ban Breathnach

The great lesson taught by the daily lives of the Essenes is their mastery of time management. Time is a finite resource toward the purpose of personal evolution. Being continuously intentional in thought, compassionate in word, and mindful in deed, the Essenes developed a state of higher consciousness within themselves throughout the continuity of their daily routine.[97]

And it wasn't just that they used the time they had wisely. They made (created, generated, extended, and compounded) time. In every aspect of their life. Their state of communion and peace imbued every task in which they engaged, increasing their overall health and peace, which lengthened their lifespan (in multiples of their contemporaries) and shortened their end-of-life disease-span, making the productive portion of their life much longer than that of others.

They lived in self-sufficient agricultural cooperatives, relieving their financial stresses, diminishing workloads, and increasing their productivity. The average Essene spent around four hours per morning tending their garden, which provided their food needs. During this time, they meditated, communed with the forces of nature, and nurtured peace in their Being.

After these morning hours of gardening, they spent the remainder of the day engaging in various activities designed to contribute toward their personal evolution, such as: moderate exercise and playful sport to nurture their physical self; assisting others in need and mentoring younger initiates to nurture their emotional self; and studying, writing, and engaging in intellectual discourse to nurture their mental self.

They fed the hungry, clothed the naked, healed the sick, counseled the hopeless, and taught the ignorant. And because their needs were met by their self-sustaining and simple agricultural lifestyle, they did not ask for compensation in return. This mindset of charity further elevated their personal evolution. Everything they did functioned as a 'peace feedback loop'; reinforcing and expanding their capacity to evolve their Being; experiencing oneness with their Higher Self; and communing with the Source, the One Law, the All Father.

You might say, "That's easy for them. They could do that. But I have responsibilities. I have bills and debts. I have built a career. I have a family to provide for." We think this way because we fail to see the continuity of the human experience. We see the lives of the Ancients as being different from those of our own. As if the human condition has changed over time, where things that were possible at one time in the distant past certainly do not hold in today's world.

Most Essenes (barring those born into the sect) were once work-a-day citizens, stuck in the grind of making a living, in careers they took years to build, and many with families to feed. The decision to 'stop the madness,' realign their priorities, and eliminate the material desires afforded them by their engagement in mainstream society was a painstaking, conscious, intentional crossroads they each had to confront.

The exchange of material burdens for immaterial peace. The trade-off between personal savings for old age and belonging to a community which would support them when that time came. The busywork and bureaucracy of societal norms and expectations versus the simplicity of seeking inward expansion and evolution. Their choice was no less daunting. Times have not changed as much as we like to think. This choice between the comforts and acceptance of mainstream society versus the simple nonmaterialistic pursuit of peace and wellbeing has been consistent since shortly after our ancestors surpassed the earliest days of 'survival mode.'

The Essenes (and the Ancients before them) were superior managers of time because they were regimented in their daily routine, facilitating efficiency of the healing and peace processes within their Being. The more regimented your daily routine, especially in the areas of eating and sleeping, the healthier and more resistant to disease your biological organism will become.[98]

Like the plant life all around you, your body (Acting Body and Feeling Body) is limited in its capacity for higher consciousness. It is by definition your Lower Self, connected most directly to the earth and its elements. It serves a divine role in your personal evolution, but it - in and of itself - is not the means of experiencing the Higher Self. That role is filled by the process of perfecting your body, emotions, and mind collaterally; the mind sharing in the nature of Spirit.

I use this analogy with plant life so that you may consider the body as a garden (as the Ancients did) requiring proper exposure to sunlight, air, water, and earth. Plants and your biological self are related in their physical nature, even sharing DNA.[99] Tend the garden of your body with care. Plants like routine. This is what science refers to as 'biorhythm.' They thrive in it. So does your biological self.[100]

As a template guide to accommodating your daily routine to one that facilitates peace, we will outline that of the Essenes (and by extension the Ancients before them, from whom they modeled their lifestyle and philosophies). This outline does not address the minutia of one's daily activities. It serves only to suggest a framework around which you might consider modifications to your existing routine.

Essenes Daily Routine Framework

Upon waking, before dawn, one does not rise hastily, but thoughtfully acknowledges the new day. Gathering oneself, thanking the Creator for granting another day in which to continue perfecting the Acting Body, Feeling Body, and Thinking Body along the process of personal evolution.

Once out of bed, one partakes in cold water ablutions (ritual washings of the body), mindfully venerating the physical and reconsecrating it to acts of service to God (the Source) and Man (others in one's sphere).

35

At daybreak, one communes with the angels of the Earthly Mother (the natural forces; see 'communions and contemplations'), absorbing their energies into the depths of one's Being.

After morning Communions, one engages in stretching and calisthenics to invigorate and strengthen the muscular, cardiovascular, respiratory, and nervous systems; incorporating rhythmic deep breathing.

Following the morning stretches and calisthenics, one tends to the work of the Garden (see notes below), remaining in a state of awareness of the morning Communion and how it applies in the expression of one's work, until the sun is highest in the sky.

At this point, one prepares for the noon meal by cleansing oneself (ablutions) and entering into Contemplations (see 'communions and contemplations'). This is done in silence, reverence, and with deep connection to the object of contemplation.

The noon meal is observed in silence (or "orderly and agreeable discourse"), reverence, and with a continued spirit of contemplation.

Following the noon meal, the day is more flexible. Considerations include but are not limited to: offering of one's time and resources to others in need, intuitive contemplation and writing, creative work, the study of the creative works of mankind and nature, and/or engaging in physical activity in sport or friendly contest. These pursuits assist in elevating one's personal evolution and are to be engaged as one's Higher Self leads. The Essenes did not consider this time as leisure, but as work toward their personal evolution. And they took it very seriously - as sacred.

At sunset, one prepares for the evening meal, again by ablutions and Communion. This time one communes with the angels of the Heavenly Father (the cosmic forces; see 'communions and contemplations'), absorbing their energies into the depths of one's Being.

The evening meal is observed in silence (or "orderly and agreeable discourse"), reverence, and with a continued spirit of communion.

Following the evening meal, one reflects on the teachings of the Ancients and/or counsels with the Elders.

Immediately before bed, one contemplates the day past and the day to come, and thanks the All Father for the gift of another day in which to grow closer to the ultimate state of communion - holistic Peace. One exudes a sense of love, power, joy, and peace in one's Being toward all persons, places, and things in their sphere of influence prior to entering into sleep. This is best done under the stars, engaging in deep rhythmic breathing.

Sleep is when the 'unknown angels' (as they were called by the Essenes) minister to oneself, healing and making whole one's body, emotions, and mind. For this reason, sleep is most important to one's peace and wellbeing.

This concludes one's day.[101]

Simplification of your life will reduce stress and increase peace. Simplified schedule. Simplified social network. Simplified food choices. Simplified material possessions. We could go on and on with areas of consideration and applications of simplicity in our modern technological, materialistic, and egotistical lives, but every choice can be resolved with two basic questions: (1) Which choice is more beneficial to my personal evolution as a biological creature, a member of the human race, and a resident of this planet? And (2) Which choice is most aligned with the Path of Peace in my life?

The Ancients taught that we should always ask our Higher Self for guidance (some know this practice as 'prayer'). If we present the 'tough questions' and most difficult decisions to our innermost consciousness prior to sleeping, we often find that the answers tend to present themselves to us unequivocally upon waking. We may not like the answer. It may not have been what our Lower Self was hoping for; but, our Higher Self is just waiting for us to be open and receptive to what it has to say in directing us toward the right and true.

The following are general guidelines which many of the Ancients, in varying degrees, followed for more effective and efficient physical health and peace. These are ideals. Do what you can to accommodate these choices in your own pursuit of the Paths of Wisdom and Peace. Even minor adjustments in your

38

behaviors, habits, and ways of thinking will reap rewards toward your personal evolution.

GENERAL GUIDELINES
for PEACE with the BODY

INGESTION

What you put into your body is the single most important contribution you make to your physical health.[102] Nothing else even comes close to the effects that food and other ingested substances have on your body, emotions, and mind. The 'Standard American Diet' of ultra-processed foods, added sugar, fat, and sodium is a recipe for disastrous health consequences.[103]

Grow it - Pick it - Eat it. This is the simplest and most healthy approach to food.[104] If you grow it, you know the quality of the soil and water used. Even the *process* of growing your own plants is therapeutic. Eating what grows locally and organically is the best scenario for your body. Packaging, shipping, storing,[105] freezing,[106] and cooking[107] of foods can deplete nutritional value; not to mention the deluge of chemicals and other toxins which are used in order for the food you purchase to be profitable to the producers, some of whom may be on the other side of the continent (or the planet).[108] This applies to animal products such as meat and dairy, as well. Processed meats are devastating to your long-term health.[109]

The Ancients largely followed a plant-based diet (a pescatarian diet was second-most practiced; and for

39

others, the meat they did eat was in very small portions and was required to pass very high health and purity standards). There are a multitude of scientific studies which can attest to the health benefits of abstaining from or reducing the consumption of meat.[110] Having been raised in the South (United States), I can attest to how challenging it is to (1) eliminate the craving for meat, and (2) to eat away from home when trying to eat healthy. If you can't stop eating meat, at the very least reduce the amount of meat you eat. Your body and the planet will thank you (yes, the adverse effect on our planet of industrial meat production is catastrophic[111]).

The Ancients taught their followers to not eat if upset or stressed. Eat slowly. Chew food until it is liquid in your mouth. Breathe deeply between mouthfuls. Eat only to two-thirds capacity (not until full). They tended not to eat more than two sizable meals per day, when the sun was highest in the sky and at sundown (no later than 8 P.M.).

EXPOSURE TO NATURE

The Ancients exposed their bodies to nature and the natural forces of sun, air, water, and earth routinely, and at the very least, once every day. And when I say exposure, I mean nearly total. Living near natural water sources (such as rivers, streams, ponds, lakes, seas, or oceans) the Ancients could expose their nearly bare bodies to nature: submersed in the water, toes in the mud, cheeks in the breeze, and basking in the sun. They tended to live in remote or obscured areas where this action wouldn't tend to cause offense.[112] For many of us, who live in cities or towns and have neighbors, this is not an acceptable option. The alternative is to expose yourself daily to the degree that your local sensibilities (and laws) will allow. Do not overexpose, especially to the sun, as this can be as bad as no exposure at all. In addition to daily exposure to nature, as you can fit into your routine, finding or making opportunities to spend time outdoors on weekends and holidays is strongly recommended.

MODERATION

Less really is more, as far as your health and peace are concerned. The Ancients practiced moderation in diet, in physical exertion, in emotional excitation, and in social interactions, among many other facets of life. In our modern society, it seems many of us try to cram as much into our schedules as possible, for fear we (or more likely our child) might miss out on a 'great opportunity,' appear unambitious to others, or a host of other neuroses. As our 'busy-ness' decreases, our peacefulness tends to increase.[113] The best thing a parent can model for their children is peace.

RHYTHMIC BREATHING

The Ancients routinely practiced deep, rhythmic breathing - when exercising, engaging in Communions and Contemplations, before and during eating, and at night before going to bed. Scientific research points out the following benefits of practicing rhythmic breathing: (1) reduced anxiety, (2) improved sleep, (3) weight loss, (4) anger management.[114]

When practicing deep rhythmic breathing, consider the quality of the air. It does make a difference. If you are breathing polluted or compromised air, you are better off not engaging in deep-breathing exercises. Try to find a 'green' area with lots of plants and trees, and which is exposed to fresh air and sunlight. Increased levels of fresh oxygen improve the benefits of deep breathing.

If you live in a city apartment or some similar habitat amidst concrete and large buildings, consider raising your own indoor garden of sprouts and baby greens near which to practice deep breathing. Even houseplants will increase oxygen content.

BEING PRESENT

In everything they did, the Ancients remained mindful of the moment. They focused on what was directly in front of them, their present experience, and the 'divine' within the mundane. They fostered an attitude of awe and amazement at the intricacies and majesty of nature and the creative works of man. They saw beauty in all things. They strove to remain simple, innocent, sincere, and compassionate as a mode of Being.

This act of 'being present' is an attribute that Science finds in the healthiest, most peaceful people,[115] especially those living to be active and healthy late in life. It is practiced still today among yogis, spiritual icons, and mindfulness experts.

If you struggle to find a point of focus that keeps you 'present' during meditation, then concentrate on your breathing. The 'communions and contemplations' section of this book offers a wealth of concepts which not only facilitate peace but increase your personal evolution, as well.

Mindfulness does not have to occur while seated yogi-style, palms pressed, eyes closed. This is a version, for certain. And it likely is the most common image people conjure when the idea of meditation comes to mind. But being 'in the moment,' being present, comes in all shapes and forms, and serves an adjacent purpose. One of the major benefits of exercising, listening to or (especially) performing music, being intimate with your partner, engaging in lively conversation, playing a sport or game, being immersed in nature, reading a good book, or any host of other pursuits is that these and other instinctual and autonomic activities facilitate Being Present. (Activities can be angels, too!).

> Notice that *not* included in this list is: being on your cell phone or mobile device. This act does not engage the mind and spirit in the same way and certainly does not tend to increase peace.

This is not to imply that traditional meditation doesn't serve a purpose. One's personal evolution still requires frequent stillness. The quieting of the mind and a regiment of focus, awareness, and introspection is not idealized in 'Activity-Based Meditation' techniques (what experts refer to as 'Mindfulness, the informal practice of being present and accepting, as opposed to the more formal 'Mindfulness Meditation'). For that, one really does need to be still, intensely focused, and not distracted by overt activity.

One of my favorite mantras is: Be Here Now. I love all three of these words. And I love them even more in combination. Being present is critical to your personal evolution and to experiencing your Higher Self. The Higher Self, which exists in the Abstract, where there is no space and no time, only experiences Being, Here, and Now. The Abstract (or Spirit), which is the essence and progenitor of Nature (as established earlier), is the ultimate reality. And, according to this logic, in the ultimate reality, the only state of existence is: Be. Here. Now.

The next section, 'weekly self-inventory,' was practiced by the Essenes as an exercise, once per week, to evaluate their progress toward personal evolution. Addressed every Sabbath (Friday evening) at sundown, it was one's first act of reconsecration of Self each week toward acts of service to the All Father and Mankind.

weekly self-inventory
the ancients' ideals of personal evolution

A great man is always willing to be little.
-   Ralph Waldo Emerson

The 'weekly self-inventory'[116] is contemplated prior to observance of the Sabbath Communion each Friday. Read the following aloud and then contemplate the answers to the questions below, trying to be as personally honest as possible, without justification or excuse.

Following the Sabbath meal, the Essenes would fast for 24 hours, instead of the normal 16. While fasting, one would only ingest water and natural fruit juices.

There is no such state as neutrality within fields of operation. Either one is operating with inferior forces or superior ones, whether knowingly or unknowingly.

Analyze your thoughts, words, and deeds. To what extent are you utilizing superior forces, or deviating from them? Evaluate your character, abilities, and physical condition. Consider your strong and weak points. This analysis will allow you to determine your role in the universal order as well as the progress of your individual evolution. Intentionally strive to align your thoughts, feelings, and actions with their highest potentials. This will further your life-time job of self-improvement, the ultimate goal of which is union with the Heavenly Father.

Alignment with the natural and cosmic forces[117] is crucial to your health and psychological balance. The process of personal evolution is to be continuously pursued and can only be conducted by the individual himself. Perfection is not demanded; simply the daily pursuit of growth within one's relationship to each force, increasing one's alignment with their energies over time.

The itemization of forces, as listed below, is solely for the purpose of expressing clearly their value and power in one's life. No artificial or rigid system of division is implied between the forces, as they act in concert under the One Law. These are divided into eight earthly forces (sun, water, air, food, man, earth, health, and joy) and eight cosmic forces (power, love, wisdom, the preserver, the Creator, eternal life, work, and peace).

As you evaluate your growth and relationship to each force from the previous week, consider each from three different aspects:

1. Is the force understood?
2. Do I feel the significance of the force deeply and sincerely?
3. Is the power used continually and in the best possible way?

The Earthly Forces...

- How much contact with **the sun** did I have? Did I utilize its solar power to the utmost every day?
- Did I drink enough **water** and begin each day with a cold-water ablution?

46

- Did I spend enough time outside, breathing clean **air**, exposing myself to the energies within the atmosphere?
- Did I eat nutrient **foods** in the right proportions?
- Did I use every moment to further my personal evolution? Did I continually strive to maximize my opportunities for serving **mankind**?
- Did I strive to grow in knowledge of the **earth**, seeking the most effective and efficient ways to grow food, and practice a healthy sexual life?
- Did I strive to appreciate the value of good **health** in my own life and in that of others? Was I intentional in forming healthy habits in my thoughts, feelings, and actions?
- Did I strive to pursue my daily tasks with a profound feeling of **joy**? Did I strive to project this joy to all those around me?

The Cosmic Forces...

- To what extent was I conscious of the **power** that I have to perform good deeds? Did I strive to be aware of how my position, personality, and surroundings are the result of past actions and that my future will be the result of my present ones?
- Did I speak gentle and kind words, expressing **love** to those around me, affecting my health, as well as the health and happiness of others? Did I strive to maintain sincerity, charity, and good will toward others, without condition, utilizing positive and encouraging feelings and words?
- Did I manifest **wisdom** in my life by practicing good thoughts? Did I strive to increase understanding

and knowledge as much as possible, maintaining only the highest of thoughts? Did I strive to understand my role in the cosmic order?

- Did I strive to **preserve** those things which have value? Did I strive to prevent the deterioration of good things? Did I use every opportunity to prevent damage to whatever has value?
- Did I use my **creative powers** to their utmost? Did I contribute originality and creativity in my efforts, especially those which might benefit others?
- Did I strive to exhibit sincerity at all times with myself in all that I do and with all others whom I meet? Did I analyze with deep sincerity my relationship with, knowledge of, and use of the forces? Did I make every effort to evaluate myself honestly, without rationalization or justification, thus contributing toward my personal evolution (**eternal life**)?
- Did I conduct my daily tasks with care and efficiency? Did I strive to feel a deep sense of satisfaction with my **work**? Did I strive to contribute to society all that I receive from it?
- Did I create and maintain **peace** within and around myself so that I might help to prevent inharmony, enmity, and conflict? Did I strive to feel a deep sense of peace and to improve the condition of everything with which I came into contact?

This 'weekly self-inventory,' as detailed above, is essential to one's personal evolution. In this way, the one, being an atom of the whole, contributes to both their own personal evolution and to that of humanity. When the many practice this, the Path of Peace, the 'kingdom of heaven' will be among us. This was Jesus' message, and that of the Ancients before him.

The next section contains the Essenes' prescribed 'communions and contemplations,' which were practiced daily.

communions and contemplations
for peace with the mind and emotions

All that we are is the result of what we have thought.

- the Buddha

OVERVIEW

The choice of wording used in this adaptation of the Essenes' 'communions and contemplations' has been mainstreamed and secularized to be more accessible to a larger audience.[118] The concepts are derived from nature and common experience, not in any one faith tradition, so universalizing the language is not antithetical. This is the only point of departure from their original expression.

You will find that the choice of wording is poetic and symbolic. As was the original. And highly so. The Essenes' use of 'flowery,' exaggerated language (much of which was not foreign in the very religious climate of Judaism of their day) served to facilitate memorization and to separate the act of Communion from the user's everyday language. The choice of vocabulary affects mental processes and, by extension, receptivity of the body. The point of the 'communions' is to raise one's level of consciousness. To that end, using elevated and lofty language and appealing to personifications of the forces of nature and the cosmos facilitates this awakening and expansion of Self.

Again, the language is poetic. It is symbolic. And it is effective.

COMPONENTS

The **bold centered heading** is the overarching focus of each communion. If all you had was this focus, you could meditate accordingly, as during meditation you want the mind as quiet as possible; allowing the Communion to penetrate your Self fully, contemplating its meaning in your Being, as well as its relation to the planet and the cosmos.

The **'Contemplative'** is a suggested additional focal point to reinforce the object of the Communion or Contemplation.

The **'Force'** is the cosmic or terrestrial force with which you are communing, utilizing its power in your Acting, Feeling, and/or Thinking Bodies.

For most who were raised in Western cultures, the idea of expanding one's consciousness to the scale of the planet or cosmos is foreign – even bizarre. We tend to think very locally about our existence and experience. Whereas many who were brought up in Eastern cultures tend to think this way as a matter of course. Localization is a restriction on yourself and on the energies which exist throughout nature and the cosmos. These energies, or forces, do not restrict themselves in this way.

If you want to experience oneness with the Source, the creative force of the universe, you will need to expand your consciousness. This is a 'muscle' which requires exercise. It will not happen in one or two meditative sittings. It is a process with which you must be patient, if in fact you wish to commune directly and intimately with your Higher Self and, by extension, the One Law, the All Father, God.

SUGGESTED PROCESS

1. Begin each Communion or Contemplation by **stating aloud the paragraph in quotes**, found immediately after the 'Force.' The resonance of the spoken words helps to facilitate mental focus and has effects within the body. If your particular situation does not allow you to feel comfortable reciting aloud, a focused thought will suffice.

2. Then **read the suggested meditations** (aloud is always preferable). Note: The A.M. and P.M. Communions each have several expressions of focus and the 'Noon Contemplations' tend to be lengthy. When time is limited, read one bullet point (Communions) or paragraph (Contemplations), then begin meditation, cycling through these over several weeks.

3. After reading all suggested meditations, **begin focused meditation** (eyes opened or closed is a personal preference and may vary from session to session or moment to moment). It's not important that you remember every word of the suggested meditations, just that you have prepared your thoughts to follow that train and that you focus on the object of communion (in the Communion that immediately follows, the *Heavenly Father* is the object of meditation).

4. It usually takes some time for the mind to quiet. It helps to begin with a short period of **deep, rhythmic breathing**, focusing on the act of breathing itself. (I use my heartbeat as the measure of breathing, inhaling for 4 beats, exhaling for 6. If I feel capable, I hold my breath with each inhale and each exhale for an additional 4 beats.) Once finding a mental 'quiet place,' a place of mindful stillness, try to remain there, striving to feel the resonance of the intention within your immediate Self, gradually expanding your sense of Self further and further, engulfing the Earth, and eventually the totality of the Cosmos.

5. Once you feel you have reached some level of inner connection with your Spirit Body (the aggregate of your Acting, Feeling, and Thinking Bodies), **recite the concluding statement** (found in quotes after the suggested meditations). As a final thought, acknowledge a sense of gratefulness to the object of the Communion for sustaining you and for assisting your personal evolution.

ICONS

The 'communions and contemplations' include chakra icons (as detailed in the graphic below). Two chakra icons are used with each meditation. All of the chakras are actually affected by each meditation, just as all of the forces or nature and the cosmos are simply manifestations of the One Law, but the icons serve as a quick guide to the primary centers of each meditation, on which you should focus for more effective concentration of energies. Within a one-week cycle, you will have accessed the energies of each of the seven chakras six times.

weekly rotation of prescribed
communions and contemplations

Friday P.M. Communion (Sabbath) – The Heavenly Father

Contemplative = The Creative Force of All Things

Force = Harmony with All Things

"I enter into the stream of everlasting and boundless Peace, aligning myself with the One Law of Creation which is the source of all things material and immaterial, the Earth from which my body is formed, and those enlightened souls who have come before me; accepting with humility the wisdom found in the forces of Nature and the Cosmos to which I have access, and holding in esteem others who strive to perfect their own personal evolution."

Then meditate on the Heavenly Father, with whom you are about to commune, contemplating his meaning and purpose in your own life and body.

- Contemplate the totality of Cosmic Laws.
- Contemplate that the Universe is a process of continuous creation in which man must take his part.
- Seek only superior thoughts so that Higher Consciousness can be achieved.

- Strive to develop an active mindset of creativity of which Love is the highest form of Creative Energy in your life and surroundings.
- Strive to attain your final goal – harmony with the One Law.

"The Heavenly Father and I are one."

 Saturday A.M. Communion – Earthly Mother

Contemplative = Food

Force = Nutrition

"I enter into the stream of everlasting and boundless Peace, aligning myself with the One Law of Creation which is the source of all things material and immaterial, the Earth from which my body is formed, and those enlightened souls who have come before me; accepting with humility the wisdom found in the forces of Nature and the Cosmos to which I have access, and holding in esteem others who strive to perfect their own personal evolution."

Then meditate on the Earthly Mother, with whom you are about to commune, contemplating her meaning and purpose in your own life and body.

Meditate on the following:

- Strive for union between your body and the nutrients of the earth by being mindful of the relationship between those elements and your physical health.
- Contemplate the meaning and importance of natural foods produced by the earth and their paramount role in health and vitality.
- Strive for awareness of the process of metabolism within your body.
- Be mindful of the powerful energies within your foods, contemplating their conservation in your body.

"The Earthly Mother and I are one.
She gives the food of life to my whole body."

Saturday Noon
Contemplation – Peace with
All Creation

"In the One Law,
which is formless,
but which contains all forms,
let us find Peace;
and uniting with the process of Creation,
let us seek Harmony with all things."

The Universe, the entire Cosmos, is the process of Creation itself. It is subject to the One Law, the culmination of all laws. All that exists is bound to the One Law. The One Law is ubiquitous, underlying all which is seen and unseen. The Law is formless, encompassing all knowledge, love, and power. It continuously unveils all truth and reality. It is mankind's guide, showing him what he must do, know, and be in order to increase his personal evolution. This kind of intuition and clarity is achievable only if one lives in harmony with the One Law.

Peace with the One Law means sustaining one's highest state of consciousness, communing at all times with superior thought currents. Through this peace, one contacts all superior forces. Through it one attains communion with these forces. Through this peace one unites with the highest of ideals. Through this peace superior intuition is awakened. Through this peace man contacts his Creator, the Source of all that is; the conscious, willful intelligence which is found within the fabric of the Universe. This peace facilitates one's personal evolution. It brings him abundance and joy. It is his purpose.

Mankind is an inseparable part of Creation. He is inextricably bound within it. He imagines himself as being separate from it because he is self-aware, though his senses are dull to the critical symbiosis he holds within it. He has become self-aware and self-serving beyond the point where these serve to preserve his life.

This sense of separation causes a feeling of lack, of limitation. In his mind he has created an illusional barrier between himself and nature, from the sources of energy abundant around him. He has severed himself from what sustains him. These sources of energy are both material and immaterial, including the tangible visible needs of physical existence as well as the invisible but sustaining needs of will, vitality, power, and - most critically - love. Mankind must evolve to his highest self, his highest state of consciousness, of his own will. To do so, it is essential for mankind to commune with these immaterial forces in order to achieve harmony with the One Law.

The Universe is a singularity consisting of all love, life, knowledge, power, and substance. It is the convergence of all things material and immaterial. It is the manifestation of all love, which imbues it, for Love is the superior force which binds all things together, from the smallest subatomic particle to the Universe itself.

One's highest self, their fullness of being, consists of three parts: the Acting Body (material body), the Feeling Body (the emotions), and the Thinking Body (the mind). These parts contribute to one's higher consciousness, which is but a ripple in the fabric of the Universe.

Saturday P.M. Communion –
Angel of Eternal Life

Contemplative = Superior Planets

Force = Overcoming Gravity

"I enter into the stream of everlasting and boundless Peace, aligning myself with the One Law of Creation which is the source of all things material and immaterial, the Earth from which my body is formed, and those enlightened souls who have come before me; accepting with humility the wisdom found in the forces of Nature and the Cosmos to which I have access, and holding in esteem others who strive to perfect their own personal evolution."

Then meditate on the Angel of Eternal Life, with which you are about to commune, contemplating its meaning and purpose in your own life and body. As the following words are said, strive to achieve union with the Cosmic Ocean of Thought.

Meditate on the following:

• Eternal life is the ultimate goal of the Universe. Your role in this goal is to continuously increase your own personal evolution. This process has no limitations or restrictions, as the universe is an inexhaustible source of energy.

• Arouse your intuitive knowledge of the eternal nature of the universe and your own unity with this continuum and the whole cosmic order.

- Contemplate the importance of overcoming gravity in the earthly currents of thought and strive to unite with the superior currents of thought in the universe. This is the highest accomplishment of man.

"Angel of Eternal Life, descend upon me and give Eternal Life to my Spirit."

 Sunday A.M. Communion – Angel of Earth

Contemplative = Top Soil, Growth

Force = Regeneration Glands

"I enter into the stream of everlasting and boundless Peace, aligning myself with the One Law of Creation which is the source of all things material and immaterial, the Earth from which my body is formed, and those enlightened souls who have come before me; accepting with humility the wisdom found in the forces of Nature and the Cosmos to which I have access, and holding in esteem others who strive to perfect their own personal evolution."

Then meditate on the Angel of Earth, with which you are about to commune, contemplating its meaning and purpose in your own life and body.

Meditate on the following:

- Contemplate the life-generating soil and the growing grass, feeling the currents of the Angel of

Earth transforming your reproductive energy into regenerative forces.

- Absorb the powers of generation and regeneration within the body to master, direct, and utilize them to regenerate your body.

    "Angel of Earth, enter my generative organs
    and regenerate my whole body."

 Sunday Noon Contemplation –Peace with the Kingdom of the Earthly Mother

"In the One Law,
which is formless,
but which contains all forms,
let us find Peace;
and to the Earth, source of all life,
profound Joy."

This Peace focuses on the unity of mankind with nature. All are governed by these forces. One's degree of alignment with nature determines her health, well-being, and vitality. This not only applies to the individual, but to mankind as a collective on this planet.

Vitality and prosperity of a nation flourish when its people live a simple existence and follow natural laws. One's restricted, unnatural, technological, and separated life creates a barrier between her and nature. Alignment with natural law is the basis of humankind's thriving on the planet. This law of unity should serve as one's guiding principle of daily life.

One should strive to serve as a nurturer, a gardener, whose mastery of sunshine, air, water, and soil keep her in constant contact with the natural forces, continuously studying their laws. Study of the book of nature is the means to peace with the Earthly Mother.

 Sunday P.M. Communion – Angel of Creative Work

Contemplative = Bees

Force = Creative Work of Man

"I enter into the stream of everlasting and boundless Peace, aligning myself with the One Law of Creation which is the source of all things material and immaterial, the Earth from which my body is formed, and those enlightened souls who have come before me; accepting with humility the wisdom found in the forces of Nature and the Cosmos to which I have access, and holding in esteem others who strive to perfect their own personal evolution."

Then meditate on the Angel of Creative Work, with which you are about to commune, contemplating its meaning and purpose in your own life and body.

Meditate on the following:

- Contemplate the great things which have been created by human labor, the great masterpieces of literature, art, science, philosophy, and everything man has created as a superstructure on nature; the highest thoughts brought forth by previous generations and inherited by the present one.
- Contemplate the importance of creative work and its paramount role in your personal evolution.
- Strive to be open to the intuitions embedded within the creative works of humankind, using their power to access your own higher intuitions.
- Creative work is the most adequate expression of love.

"Angel of Creative Work, descend upon humanity and give abundance to all men."

 Monday A.M. Communion – Angel of Life

Contemplative = Trees

Force = Vitality, Life Force

"I enter into the stream of everlasting and boundless Peace, aligning myself with the One Law of Creation which is the source of all things material and immaterial, the Earth from which my body is formed, and those enlightened souls who have come before me; accepting with humility the wisdom found in the

64

forces of Nature and the Cosmos to which I have access, and holding in esteem others who strive to perfect their own personal evolution."

Then meditate on the Angel of Life, with which you are about to commune, contemplating its meaning and purpose in your own life and body.

Meditate on the following:

• Strive to become aware of the life, health, and vitality in your body and of that of the planet, and the dynamic relationship between them.

• Contemplate the energies of the living force around you, allowing you to distribute them to your body as needed.

"Angel of Life, enter my limbs
and give strength to my whole body."

 **Monday Noon
Contemplation – Peace with
Culture**

"In the One Law,
which is formless,
but which contains all forms,
let us find Peace;
to our knowledge,
Wisdom."

Masterpieces of art, architecture, music, literature, *et al.* embody mankind's pinnacle of wisdom from antiquity, up to and including the present. One can only achieve his pre-ordained place in the cosmic order by absorbing the highest knowledge of mankind, translated through the great teachings of those enlightened before us. These masterpieces represent one-third of all knowledge.

There are three pathways to finding truth – the path of intuition which was followed by the sages and prophets; the path of nature, that of the scientist; and the path of culture, that of the great masterpieces of literature and the arts. Study of the masterpieces of mankind is to be conducted via intuition and nature. Discovery through intuition means that one endeavors to comprehend the intuitions of the creative genius, effectively increasing one's own personal evolution. Discovery via nature means finding corollaries of their wisdom within nature. By making this ongoing comparison, and by engaging one's own intuition, personal evolution is advanced.

It is the duty of everyone to elevate their personal evolution by way of the creative works of previous generations, so that the intuitions of past masters can be expanded into the future, thus increasing mankind's evolution as a species. It is mankind's obligation to continue the work of the Creator on the planet, thus becoming co-Creator with the Source. Universal culture is important to human and personal evolution because it represents the highest ideals which mankind has held, and an all-sided synthesis of knowledge of the problems of life and their right solution.

This knowledge was brought forth by highly evolved individuals, masters who had the power to contact the universal sources of knowledge, energy, and harmony which exist in the Cosmic Ocean of Thought. The truths in these masterpieces are eternal. They come from the one eternal unchanging source of all knowledge. Such teachings belong to no one school of thought or religion. All great sacred writings of mankind, from every culture, teach the same ageless wisdom. Apparent contradictions come from the limitations and narrow-mindedness of followers who misinterpret, misunderstand, and/or misconstrue the teachings of the Ancients.

The purpose of study is not to garner additional information, but to open one to the sources of universal truth. When one contemplates a great work of humanity, the concepts, images, sensations, and symbols of letters and words themselves create in the Thinking Body powerful vibrations and currents of thought. These vibrations and currents put the individual in touch with the Thinking Body of the great master who gave forth the truth. This provides an infinite source of understanding, wisdom, and harmony accessible by no other means. This is the profound importance, the esoteric revelation, of Peace with Culture.

Monday P.M. Communion –
Angel of Peace

Contemplative = Mindfulness

Force = Peace Within

"I enter into the stream of everlasting and boundless Peace, aligning myself with the One Law of Creation which is the source of all things material and immaterial, the Earth from which my body is formed, and those enlightened souls who have come before me; accepting with humility the wisdom found in the forces of Nature and the Cosmos to which I have access, and holding in esteem others who strive to perfect their own personal evolution."

Then meditate on the Angel of Peace, with which you are about to commune, contemplating its meaning and purpose in your own life and body.

Meditate on the following:

- Your own deep inner intuition of peace within you and the infinite universe.
- The essence of true peace is the Path of Spirituality, which is the purpose of life.
- Your most immediate duty is to create peace within yourself and with everything around you. That work of peace begins from within.

"Peace, peace, peace,
Angel of Peace,
Be always everywhere."

 **Tuesday A.M. Communion –
Angel of Joy**

Contemplative = Beauty

Force = Harmony

"I enter into the stream of everlasting and boundless Peace, aligning myself with the One Law of Creation which is the source of all things material and immaterial, the Earth from which my body is formed, and those enlightened souls who have come before me; accepting with humility the wisdom found in the forces of Nature and the Cosmos to which I have access, and holding in esteem others who strive to perfect their own personal evolution."

Then meditate on the Angel of Joy, with which you are about to commune, contemplating its meaning and purpose in your own life and body.

Meditate on the following:

• Contemplate all forms of natural beauty, absorbing joy from them: sunrise, sunsets, mountains, flowers, colors, aromas, etc.

• Contemplate attainment of inner harmony and serenity.

"Angel of Joy, descend upon Earth
And give beauty to all things."

Tuesday Noon
Contemplation – Peace with
Humanity (Social Peace)

"In the One Law,
which is formless,
but which contains all forms,
let us find Peace;
to humanity, our brothers and sisters,
the blessing of Work."

Peace with Humanity refers to equanimity between peoples, to societal and economic harmony. Injustices between people occur due to deviations from the Law. Deviations include wealth and poverty, rulers and slaves, and social enmity. Great wealth is concentrated into the hands of the few because of man's exploitation of man. This imbalance creates misery for the oppressor and the oppressed. The multitude feels hatred and the few feel fear. On the other hand, one is impoverished due to inferior thoughts, feelings, and actions. Lacking and excess are both deviations from natural law.

Escape from this circle of oppression is achieved only through educating the ignorant in the world. This must be a continuous process. Teaching and example, administered by a Master, can assist the individual in guiding principles, but the Master cannot change an individual. The individual herself has to do the changing; nobody else can do it for her. If a person is in alignment with natural laws, strives to understand them, and intentionally operates within them, she will experience no lack. She will maintain balance and harmony in her life and will find her needs met.

Rid yourself of all excess. What you do not need, give to those who have need. Your nourishment and material needs can be provided without struggle through proper alignment with natural laws. Practice order, efficiency, and individual freedom in all things. Strive to be practical, spiritual, and intellectual in your endeavors. Take no part in politics or military service. Neither can change man's chaotic condition. Exploitation and oppression of others is completely unnecessary.

Maintain your own small house and a garden sufficient for your needs. Take part in communal activities wherever your service is needed. Be agriculturally proficient, espousing knowledge of plants, soil conditions, and climate.

Nature is your bible. The process of gardening is your teacher, informing you of the processes inherent in the universe, unveiling its secrets. Read and study the great book of nature continuously. It is a source of unending knowledge, energy, and peace. When you garden, you are in communion with life itself, as well as the angels of sun, air, water, and earth.

Your attitude toward your work is of utmost importance. Approach it as if to uncover life's mysteries. The bounty your garden yields is only an incidental benefit of your activities; the true rewards are the vitalizing life force, the increase in knowledge, and the deep-seated peace you have gained, enriching your life. Approach gardening as a sacred task, conducting it in silence as you work, communing with nature, creating the 'kingdom of heaven' within your sphere of influence.

Your economic and social organizations are a function of your peace, not the means to it. Offer your time and energy freely to your community without the expectation of reciprocation. Through this harmony your individual evolution will progress steadily. Teach the ignorant and chasten those who deviate, according to the opportunities that present themselves to you. But do so with a spirit of love and compassion.

Peace with humanity will only be attained when the majority follow this path.

 Tuesday P.M. Communion – Angel of Power

Contemplative = Stars, Superior Acts

Force = Nervous System, Cosmic Ocean of Life

"I enter into the stream of everlasting and boundless Peace, aligning myself with the One Law of Creation which is the source of all things material and immaterial, the Earth from which my body is formed, and those enlightened souls who have come before me; accepting with humility the wisdom found in the forces of Nature and the Cosmos to which I have access, and holding in esteem others who strive to perfect their own personal evolution."

Then meditate on the Angel of Power, with which you are about to commune, contemplating its meaning and purpose in your own life and body.

Meditate on the following:

• The entire universe is a cosmic ocean of life in which currents of cosmic power are continually uniting all forms of life on all planets and connecting you with all organisms.

• Strive to become aware of the cosmo-vital forces surrounding you and within you, absorbing their energies via the nervous system to maximize your body's health and vitality.

"Angel of Power, descend upon my Acting Body
And direct all my acts."

 **Wednesday A.M.
Communion – Angel of the
Sun**

Contemplative = Sunrise

Force = Fire of Life

"I enter into the stream of everlasting and boundless Peace, aligning myself with the One Law of Creation which is the source of all things material and immaterial, the Earth from which my body is formed, and those enlightened souls who have come before me; accepting with humility the wisdom found in the forces of Nature and the Cosmos to which I have access, and holding in esteem others who strive to perfect their own personal evolution."

Then meditate on the Angel of the Sun, with which you are about to commune, contemplating its meaning and purpose in your own life and body.

Meditate on the following:

- The sun is the great living force in terrestrial nature, an ever-present source of energy, without which there would be no life.
- Meditate on the effect of solar rays which penetrate your organism at the point of the solar plexus. This point is the oldest unity in the human organism.
- Strive to become open and receptive to solar energies, establishing unity with the sun and distributing its power throughout the body.

> "Angel of the Sun, enter my Solar Center,
> And give the fire of life to my whole body."

 **Wednesday Noon
Contemplation – Peace with
the Family (Feeling Body)**

"In the One Law,
which is formless,
but which contains all forms,
let us find Peace;

to our family and friends,
Love."

Peace with the Family is a function of the Feeling Body (the emotions). Your family includes all those with whom you come into daily contact. This includes your conventional family, but extends also to friends, associates, and others within your sphere. This Peace is determined by your emotions, your control of them, and their proper expression.

The most fundamental and primordial feeling is Love. It is first experienced within the womb between a child and its mother. It is intensified upon birth through maternal bonding, through contact of skin, warmth of touch, sound of voice, and receiving of nourishment. This experience, even before birth, is the first experience we have as biological creatures. For this reason and others, Love is the truest and most peaceful expression of our Feeling Body. Love your Creator from the depths of your Being, to include your thoughts, emotions, and actions. The expression of Creative Love is life itself.

Divine Love is the dominant cosmic force. It regulates all substance, though it is manifested most effectively through the Feeling Body. The Feeling Body consists of the emotions one receives as well as those which she radiates. The Feeling Bodies of all create a planetary feeling atmosphere, invisible and imponderable, but having enormous influence and power.

Every feeling and emotion created by an individual becomes a part of the feeling atmosphere of Earth, setting up a resonance of co-vibration with all similar feelings in the earth's atmosphere. If an inferior feeling is sent out, its creator is immediately tuned in to all the similar inferior feelings in the Earth's Feeling Body. One thus opens the gate to a flood of destructive power which rushes in and seizes control of her feelings. Directly affecting the body, this force adversely affects the whole glandular system. It manifests disease cells, lowers vitality, shortens life, and results in an unlimited amount of suffering.

Most people experience inharmony and imbalance in their emotions. Innate to man, the instinct for self-preservation (buried deep in the Feeling Body through thousands of years of survival-based evolution) dominates humankind from birth and is the infant's most primitive instinct. This instinct arouses three fundamental emotions: fear, anger, and love. Fear and anger are inferior feelings; the Love feeling, while superior, is rudimentary. Self-preservation is attuned to the law of nature until the Thinking Body matures. After the Thinking Body matures, the instinct of self-preservation can serve to stunt a person's personal evolution. This is mankind's initial deviation from the Law.

When a person who has developed the capacity for mature thought allows their Feeling Body to dominate their Thinking Body, an imbalance occurs. This imbalance misaligns one's sense of harmony, creating a regressed psychological state. Instinctive impulses can only serve evolutionary progress when controlled by the thinking faculties.

Nature has given humankind the capacity to think so she may be able to understand its laws and direct her life in harmony with them. By impeding her own personal evolution, she impedes the planetary evolution of humankind. Whether deviation of the Law occurs knowingly or unknowingly makes no difference. The lack of harmony with the Law leads to self-centered, small, artificial laws of egoism, which cause walls of separation between a person and the rest of the human family, nature, and the One Law - the Source. Deviation from the Law results in suffering.

The Feeling Body can be the source of blissful health and happiness when in alignment with natural law. In its right expression of Love, humankind is tasked with the creation of the 'kingdom of heaven' in their daily life.

Peace with the Family is mankind's expression of love towards one another.

Wednesday P.M.
Communion – Angel of Love

Contemplative = Superior Feeling

Force = Emotions, Cosmic Ocean of Love

"I enter into the stream of everlasting and boundless Peace, aligning myself with the One Law of Creation which is the source of all things material and immaterial, the Earth from which my body is formed, and those enlightened souls who have come before me; accepting with humility the wisdom found in the forces of Nature and the Cosmos to which I have access, and holding in esteem others who strive to perfect their own personal evolution."

Then meditate on the Angel of Love with which you are about to commune, contemplating its meaning and purpose in your own life and body.

Meditate on the following:

- Love is the highest creative feeling.
- The Cosmic Ocean of Love is universal, binding and maintaining all things.
- Life is a manifestation of Love.
- Receive the superior currents of Love through the Feeling Body; strive to understand their importance within you and in the universe that surrounds you.
- Become conscious of and receptive to the currents of love as an infinite source of energy and power which can be concentrated and directed in all manifestations of your consciousness.
- The injury you inflict on any form of life, you also inflict upon yourself because of the dynamic unity of all life forms in the Cosmic Ocean of Love.
- Express strong feelings of love to the whole of humankind and to all forms of life on earth and in infinite space.
- Express this love for all life forms through deeds.
- Attract and send forth superior currents of love.

"Angel of Love, descend upon my Feeling Body,
And purify all my feelings."

**Thursday A.M. Communion
– Angel of Water**

Contemplative = Blood, Rivers, etc.

Force = Circulation

"I enter into the stream of everlasting and boundless Peace, aligning myself with the One Law of Creation which is the source of all things material and immaterial, the Earth from which my body is formed, and those enlightened souls who have come before me; accepting with humility the wisdom found in the forces of Nature and the Cosmos to which I have access, and holding in esteem others who strive to perfect their own personal evolution."

Then meditate on the Angel of Water, with which you are about to commune, contemplating its meaning and purpose in your own life and body.

Meditate on the following:

- The circulation of water in nature and that of blood in the body are analogues.
- All organisms consist primarily of water, which is fundamental to life.
- The quality of blood determines the health of the organism, as the quality of water determines the health of the environment.
- Contemplate the occurrences of water in nature, such as lakes, rivers, seas, etc. realizing the continuity of water systems on the planet with those

of biological life. Realize a symbiosis between the waters of the earth and those of your physical self.

"Angel of Water, enter my blood
and give the water of Life to my whole body."

Thursday Noon
Contemplation – Peace with
the Mind (Thinking Body)

"In the One Law,
which is formless,
but which contains all forms,
let us find Peace;
to our mind,
Power."

The essence of the Sevenfold Peace is based on 'Peace with the Mind.' Mind being the creator of thought. Thought is the superior life force, more powerful than either the forces of Feeling or Action, because it is the instigator of both.

The totality of your thoughts is called your Thinking Body. The totality of all the thoughts in all of the billions of thinking bodies on the Earth forms a Planetary Thinking Body. The totality of all superior thoughts in the universe forms a Cosmic Thinking Body (a.k.a. a Cosmic Ocean of Thought). Your Thinking Body has three functions: individual, planetary, and cosmic.

Your Thinking Body's function is to access the power of thought to direct the emotions and actions. Its planetary purpose is to radiate the highest of thought currents to contribute toward the evolution of humanity.

The thoughts which pass through your mind create a field around you. Your thoughts continuously radiate outward, entering the planetary stream of thought. But you are also influenced by that same stream of thought, affecting your own physical, emotional, and mental health and stability. You are responsible for the thoughts you contribute to the Planetary Thinking Body.

The cosmic function is not easily fulfilled. In order to contribute to the Cosmic Ocean of Thought (or Cosmic Thinking Body), one's thoughts must be freed from planetary gravitation. To achieve this, one must have only the highest of thought currents, superior thoughts. The fullness of the Law is represented by the Cosmic Ocean of Thought. It is the omnipotence and the omnipresence of the Law. It was before time began and it will continue after time ceases. It is the primal force. It is eternal and infinite, directing all phases of evolution, both planetary and cosmic. One's cosmic function is to create such superior currents of thought that they unite with the Cosmic Ocean of Thought. One's goal is to think 'God's' thoughts.

Humankind's Thinking Body is her most precious gift from the Creator. It grants her the means to be conscious of the Law, to comprehend it, to align with it by choice, to perceive its reflections in the material world, and to commune with it. In this way, one becomes a co-creator with the Source. No higher privilege exists in the universe.

This privilege allows one to achieve whatsoever she desires which is in accordance with the Law. This power contains within it the ability to reconcile any past inharmony, to recreate one's Thinking Body, to improve the body's healing capacity, and generate total harmony in one's sphere of influence.

Thoughts can be employed in the act of creation or destruction. Even passing thoughts have the ability to generate effects on the Feeling and Acting Bodies. These thought currents can penetrate one's being at the cellular level. These effects, whether constructive or destructive, radiate throughout the body. For this reason, creating the precondition for only the highest thoughts is critical for health and peace in the body, emotions, and mind.

Every time you accept inferior thought currents, you are welcoming negative forces into your life. Those negative forces act upon your Feeling Body. This sets up an emotional disequilibrium in your Feeling Body, which in turn acts on your Acting Body. This disequilibrium automatically causes further deviations, further inharmony, further disease in the Feeling and Acting Bodies. These create an inharmonious atmosphere around you which affects others.

Every inharmonious or inferior thought begins a cascade of deviations. This inharmony is contagious. These inharmonious thoughts can be prevented right at their source, by being conscious and aware of your stream of thought, not accepting into your thoughts any inferior or inharmonious thought.

Mankind has been elevated to the position of co-creator due to his sharing of essence with the Creator. In this elevated state, mankind may choose to align with natural and cosmic laws, increasing one's personal evolution and subsequently one's experience of peace and harmony; or to deviate from them, increasing one's misery and ill health. Peace and harmony cannot be attained by material means, technical evolution, or economic systems. The monumental amount of suffering humankind has initiated will only be overcome when it chooses to pursue harmony in its Thinking Body. This willful and intentional inward seeking of communion with the All Father on a global scale is the 'kingdom of heaven' proclaimed by the Ancients.

 ## Thursday P.M. Communion – Angel of Wisdom

Contemplative = Superior Thoughts

Force = Thinking Body

"I enter into the stream of everlasting and boundless Peace, aligning myself with the One Law of Creation which is the source of all things material and immaterial, the Earth from which my body is formed, and those enlightened souls who have come before me; accepting with humility the wisdom found in the forces of Nature and the Cosmos to which I have access, and holding in esteem others who strive to perfect their own personal evolution."

Then meditate on the Angel of Wisdom, with which you are about to commune, contemplating its meaning and purpose in your own life and body.

Meditate on the following:

- One's thoughts are felt locally, globally, and cosmically.

- A Cosmic Ocean of Thought pervades all space. It contains all thought, the highest form of cosmic energy, never fading and never failing.

- Strive to commune with the Angel of Wisdom by attuning to the thoughts of all great thinkers of humanity's past.

- Develop your ability through this resonance with the Cosmic Ocean of Thought to generate powerful currents of thought and achieve intuitive wisdom.

"Angel of Wisdom, descend upon my Thinking Body, and enlighten all my thoughts."

 Friday A.M. Communion – Angel of Air

Contemplative = Breath

Force = Energies of Atmosphere

"I enter into the stream of everlasting and boundless Peace, aligning myself with the One Law of Creation which is the source of all things material and immaterial, the Earth from which my body is formed, and those enlightened souls who have come before me; accepting with humility the wisdom found in the forces of Nature and the Cosmos to which I have

84

access, and holding in esteem others who strive to perfect their own personal evolution."

Then meditate on the Angel of Air, with which you are about to commune, contemplating its meaning and purpose in your own life and body.

Meditate on the following:

- Contemplate the dynamic unity between air and life. Respiration is the link between your organism and the cosmos.
- Where there is life, there is breath. The atmosphere around you and the air within you play a critical role in health and vitality.
- Execute deep rhythmic breathing, enabling you to utilize specific energies around you.

"Angel of Air, enter my lungs
and give the air of Life to my whole body."

 **Friday Noon Contemplation
– Peace with the Body
(Acting Body)**

"In the One Law,
which is formless,
but which contains all forms,
let us find Peace;
to our body,
Life."

Through the Acting Body are manifested all the laws of life and the cosmos. In it is to be found the key to the whole universe. Each person has three roles: strive to increase one's own individual evolution; contribute to the evolution of humankind on the planet; and become a superior point within the cosmos. The Acting Body plays a part in each role. The body is a divine creation, purposed by the Creator to facilitate one's personal evolution, in no way subordinate to any other phase of one's Being. The Acting Body is awaiting one to make intentional use of its earthly and cosmic potentials.

Each person is not an isolated being alone in the universe but belongs to a Cosmic Ocean of Thought and Life. For this reason, all Acting Bodies are inter-related and affect one another. Each person's physical health and vitality are subsequently of the highest importance, both to herself and to all others.

One of your goals in life is perfection of the Acting Body in all three of its phases (individual, planetary, and cosmic). To do so, one must strive to mold it to the forces and energies in and around oneself. Strive to learn the effects of foods and the natural forces – including sun, water, air, and earth – on your body. Begin each day with a cold-water ablution and by exposing your body to solar rays. Spend time working in the garden (or otherwise outdoors) to commune with the forces of nature.

Bodily disease is the result of deviations from the Law. Strive to learn the healing potential of herbal remedies, heliotherapy, and hydrotherapy. Ascertain the proper diet for remedying every illness. Practice deep breathing. Realize that the Thinking Body has power over the Acting and Feeling Bodies.

Practice moderation in all things. Practice fasting as a means of regenerating the body and developing the will, resulting in an increase of spiritual power. These practices bring peace and harmony to the Acting Body. But do not attach undue importance to the Acting Body. The consideration and care you give to it is solely to keep it in good health as an instrument through which you are to perform acts of wisdom and love for your fellow man. In this way, your Acting Body contributes to your personal evolution, to that of the planet, and to the cosmos. In this way, you enable yourself to become a co-creator with the One Law (the Heavenly Father).

in closing…

This ancient wisdom, founded in prehistory,
transcending place and time,
obscured by mysticism and misunderstanding,
gifted from one Enlightened to the next
over thousands of years,
has now found its way into your hands.
I hope it also finds its way into your
body, emotions, and mind.
And that you encounter your Higher Self,
your Spirit, in a very personal
and powerful way along the Path of Peace.
That your Higher Self communes with the Source,
the One Law, the All Father, the Creator, God.
And that you discover that you are
one with all Creation.
This is my hope for you, and for me,
and for all those who strive to
perfect their own personal evolution.

There is no 'them.'
There is only 'us.'

appendix i: the ancients on…
perspectives on purpose, finances,
residence, chores, and the good

The greatest wealth is to live content with little.

-   Plato

The topics touched on in this section are some of the biggest and/or most common that we face on a regular basis. While time marches on, and new societal and technological scenarios arise, the Ancients' teachings are sufficient to cover all aspects of life and living and can be applied to all situations.

If a subject you are interested in is not listed in this book or its 'communions,' ask yourself two basic questions and then let your Higher Self tackle the problem for you. It will let you know. And it probably won't take that long.

The two basic questions are:

1. Which path most increases my long-term peace?
2. Which path contributes most to my personal evolution?

Otherwise, the 'communions and contemplations' you are doing every day, three times a day (right? right? right?) usually cover the underlying tenets of peace and address more or less nuanced subjects. And as I like to say about the teachings of the Ancients, "If it ain't in there, it ain't important." Which means if you're losing sleep over something that is not addressed in the teachings of the Ancients, you're probably focused on the wrong things.

Peace can be fostered through our pursuit of the highest ideals of Purpose and Calling, Finances, Residence, Chores, and Good and Evil.

PURPOSE & CALLING

The two most important days in your life are the day you were born and the day you find out why.

- Mark Twain

There is a distinct difference between 'Purpose' and 'Calling.' Your Purpose is a function of the Source. Your Calling is a function of Humanity. For those who lack a discernable Calling, a Vocation serves the same purpose.

According to the Ancients, your Purpose is to commune with the All Father, the One Law, the Source of all substance both material and immaterial, the Creator, God. There is only one, shared universal purpose for all Beings. This is the goal of the path of your personal evolution.

Your Calling (or Vocation) is the way in which you spread love, joy, wisdom, and power to the rest of humanity. It is the means by which you serve mankind. It is the way in which you contribute to humanity's evolution.

A Calling is the presence of a deep personal drive within oneself. It is the inexplicable compulsion toward a mission or task which creates a sense of inevitability and passion deep within our Being. A Vocation serves in conjunction with, or, as an alternative to the presence of a Calling. A Vocation allows one to

91

contribute to the betterment of mankind, fulfilling one of many functional needs of humanity in the absence of a specific Calling. Both serve as a means of increasing your personal evolution.

The Ancients taught that one should be deeply grateful for having either a Calling or a Vocation (and especially to have both), as both contribute equally toward one's Purpose. There is no qualitative difference between the two. In like manner, not fulfilling a Calling is akin to not fulfilling a Vocation. These are each detrimental to one's own personal evolution and by extension the evolution of mankind.

One's Purpose never changes. One's Calling and/or Vocation can evolve and change over time. Whether you follow a Calling or a Vocation, they are each a function of Purpose.

F I N A N C E S

Neither a borrower nor a lender be.
- Shakespeare from *Hamlet*

Both states of wealth and poverty were considered by the Ancients to be deviations from the Law. One was to maintain neither of these financial states. Giving away all surpluses to those in need was how they avoided becoming excessively wealthy; and maintaining a respectable work ethic, being responsible with money, and living frugally is how they avoided poverty. To be clear, having few possessions and living a frugal life is not the same as poverty. Poverty, according to the Ancients, is the lack of even the most basic requirements of life and living, such as food, clothing, and shelter.[119]

It is easy to say that situations are more complex than this simplistic valuation, and that sometimes being 'broke' is just the result of dumb luck or an unfortunate series of circumstances. Sometimes medical situations put us in dire need. These are all harsh realities which most if not all of us experience at some point in our lives. What we are tasked with is preparing for these potential hardships by making wise life choices, sound financial decisions, and taking advantage of opportunities for earning as they present themselves. Living in community is also a way to guard against poverty. And then, once hardships occur, to maintain our resolve to meet those obligations and correct our financial situation as quickly as possible.

If you are like most people, you have experienced financial hardship at some point, but you probably can pinpoint several (if not many) financial or life choices in the past which were not prudent or responsible, the culmination of which may have exacerbated your financial hardship once tough times arrived. It is easy to take pity; it is hard to take accountability.

Where the accumulation of wealth is concerned, the ancient founders of the Peace traditions did not accumulate wealth nor savings as such. They lived well within their means, having a small residence, growing their own food, and sharing the surplus with those in need. They lived minimally to facilitate charity. Their primary financial principle was to live a frugal life so that they might be generous.

On the topic of Savings, there is a degree of savings which increases peace, and a degree of savings which diminishes it.

By at least one modern economists' standard, savings which is reasonable and prudent meets the following criteria: (1) approximately three to six months living expenses; (2) emergency funds; (3) savings toward a foreseen major purchase, such as a home, vehicle, education, or the like; and (4) retirement contributions.[120]

Beyond this, excessive savings is unrealized potential for acts of goodwill, charity, and social good. By using excess savings toward acts of kindness and philanthropy, both personal savings and philanthropic savings serve your personal evolution; the former by bringing peace to you and those that depend on you, and the latter by improving the lives of others. By reflexive logic, possessing excess savings and not using it for social good (hoarding wealth), or not having sufficient personal savings to provide for your own financial peace (living paycheck to paycheck), are both deviations[121], which must be remedied.

Being rich is not a deviation. Neither is being poor. Remaining there is.

Debt, on the other hand, has no place in the Path of Peace. It is a deviation only, according to the Ancients. Debt may bring you other things, but it is not Peace.

Many problems are caused by excessive materialism and the attachment to possessions. We live beyond our means and hold debt, squander our resources, and collect more and more things we do not need. We are aware of this issue in our culture, made clear by sayings like, "You can't take it with you," (George S. Kaufman) implying there is no lasting value in wealth and possessions past the grave. But knowing this doesn't seem to alter our less-than enlightened behavior.

Finances can contribute to our experience of peace or act as a source of unbearable stress. It is up to us to find financial peace through right thinking and right actions.

R E S I D E N C E

A house is made of walls and beams;
a home is built with love and dreams.

- unknown

A function of your peace is your living situation, in terms of geography, neighborhood, and surroundings, as well as the atmosphere within the home. Research suggests that people who live in noisy, artificially lit, busy urban areas experience more stress on a daily basis than people who live in rural settings, in and around nature.[122]

Living in a community where you have longstanding ties, where people know you by name, lend a hand in times of need, and experience social interaction, not only reduces stress, but enhances peace.[123] Small towns have higher 'happiness' ratings than big cities.[124] People who live close to family and interact with them on a regular basis experience more peace (as a rule).[125] Even quiet neighborhoods that are within a short distance of industrial or business districts have increased stress indicators.[126]

There is a direct correspondence between your living situation and your experience of peace.[127]

CHORES

What the country needs is dirtier fingernails
and cleaner minds.

- Will Rogers

The age of automation, while clever, has stolen an opportunity for peace in our lives, and often, in our family's as well. The doing of chores, such as washing the dishes, sweeping the floors, and even mowing the yard, have been otherwise delegated. One of the initial selling points of these technologies was that they 'free up time to spend with our family.'[128] Instead, what they tend to do is free up time to spend *away* from our family and foster an attitude of entitlement; off to separate rooms where yet other devices consume our time and attention.

And even if you are the only one in your household, the work of chores - the mindless tasks of scrubbing and cleaning, folding and 'toting' – is good for the soul. Chores allow time for our minds to process daily stresses. *Our hands at work and our minds at peace.* Not to mention the satisfaction of a job well done.

Menial tasks such as yardwork, laundry, dishes, dusting, etc., are better seen as opportunities to create peace in our home and in our family, not burdens to be pushed aside to automation or outsourcing. Creating time for Self or for Family does not have to include the spending of finances at entertainment or dining venues. A component of 'Peace with Self,' and of 'Peace with Family,' is in the pride of accomplishing a task, as a product of effort, of applying 'elbow grease.'

Peace with Self and with the Family happens one chore at a time.

GOOD & EVIL

I believe that unarmed truth and unconditional love
will have the final word in reality. This is why right,
temporarily defeated, is stronger than evil triumphant.
- Martin Luther King, Jr.

The Ancients did not try to eradicate Evil, that which is harmful and unjust and detrimental to oneself and to others. They focused on enhancing the Good, that which is right and just and beneficial for personal evolution. They believed that Good expanded would always suffocate Evil. And that focusing on the Evil, even for the purposes of eradication, fed it power. This phenomenon is referred to in psychology as 'Ironic Process Theory.'[129]

The light shines and the darkness cannot resist it.[130]

appendix ii: the thread
continuity and connectivity of the
ancient peace traditions

All things must come to the soul from its roots,
from where it is planted.
- St. Teresa of Avila

I refer to the 'Thread' several times throughout this book. So, for the purposes of clarity and illumination, I offer a summarization of this 'Thread,' the continuity through history of Peace traditions which influenced and contributed to the Essene philosophy and perspective. Nothing is ever as simple and easy as its explanation might lead one to believe. There are knowns and unknowns, and factors beyond our means to uncover, so we use the facts available and intuit (deduce) the rest based on what we know about historical context, tendencies, and the nature of humankind. This 'Thread' has been detailed throughout the book to this point in a rather oblique manner, so I wanted to streamline its presentation into a more easily accessible and linear form, which I am doing here.[131]

It is believed that the primary expression of spirituality throughout Prehistory (99% of human history) is **Animism** (summarized as 'spirit is in everything and, thus, everything is connected'), wherein man venerates the forces of nature and the cosmos (sun, air, water, earth, power, wisdom, joy, and love) for their life-giving sustenance. This practice is predominant up until the mid-to-late Pleistocene/early Neolithic periods (ca. 9,700 B.C.E).

Throughout the **Neolithic period** (app. 9,700 – 5,000 B.C.E.), **Totemism** (the selecting of one specific item as the object of communion) becomes prominent. This practice is made evident in cave paintings and carved figures of animals and animal chimeras. Animism and Totemism were overlapping expressions of the veneration of nature. Once the Neolithic Revolution occurred (marked by the transition from hunter-gatherer methods of food acquisition to husbandry-agricultural methods), spiritual practices were more easily centralized, organized, and formalized.

> This idea of God being imbued within Creation is a fundamental tenet of Essene teachings. In essence, all that exists is God, within whom all things reside.

Once regions were settled and peoples formed societies, the role of the **shaman/priest** became solidified as a recognized and respected authority on social conscience, mores, and spirituality. Shaman[132] (Russian, *šamán*; Tungusic *samān*; Chinese *shāmén*; and Sanskrit *śramana* – the likely origin of the word; *et al.*) were known to enter meditative trance states to commune with the Spirit world, manifesting healing powers and teachings from the immaterial realm into the material realm. These shaman were ascetics who devoted themselves to 'higher purpose,' and who were seekers of knowledge and truth.

The people of the **Indus Valley** (now known as Hindu), thought to be the formal origin of the concept of shamanism, do not document a name to the earliest form of their religion, as it was universal. There were no other known religious practices divergent from shamanism before ca. 9,700 B.C.E., so it needed not be delineated or labeled. Hinduism (not called that at the time; foreigners assigned this name to the spiritual practices of the Indus Valley civilization[133]) is thought to be the oldest known religion, dating back to the late Pleistocene and early Neolithic periods more than 12,000 years ago (and very likely closer to 40,000 years ago or more). It is thought to have been widespread throughout the Asiatic world.

cont.

The Essenes were well-known for their healing and teaching. Drawing on their continuous meditation (communion) practices, they would perform healings which many viewed as miracles. The Essenes did not claim mystical powers, but that they communed with the natural and cosmic forces to manifest such healings. Being fully open and receptive to the forces around them, they were able to use these forces to improve their health and the health of others. Jesus was considered the Essene Master, and as such was highly proficient in this area.

As a crude parallel: certain people can get things to happen that others, no matter how hard they try, can't. For instance, when I was a young 1st-year teacher at my first school district, I went into the administrative office to speak to the Superintendent. The office staff asked if I had an appointment and what it was in reference to, then asked me to sit, where I waited for quite some time. However, when Lulu (name changed to protect the innocent), who was a 30-year+ teacher and who had earned a measure of respect around the district, came in and asked to see the Superintendent (she just called him Tom – again, name changed), they sent her right in.

The difference here is in the nature of the relationship and the degree of earned respect. Commune with the forces of nature and the cosmos consistently and continuously for long enough and maybe you'll be on a 'first-name basis' with them, too, like Lulu was with Tom, but with whom I couldn't get an audience.

The Indus Valley Civilization is known to have had contact with **Egypt and Sumer** (both polytheistic societies) by around 5,000 B.C.E., wherein agricultural and cultural practices (Hinduism) were shared. This intermingling of Hindu, Sumerian, Egyptian, Mesopotamian, Babylonian, and Persian traditions is important to the formulation of the Essene's teachings via Moses.

Enoch (ca. 3049-2684 B.C.E.) is revered by the Essenes as their founder and the prophet who, taken by God before death[134], revealed the mysteries to Moses some 1,500 years later in his spiritual role as 'Metatron,' messenger of God (see the apocryphal books of *Enoch*). Other than this reference, it is difficult to see where he ties into the timeline, and what exposure he might have had to other cultures and spiritual traditions, if any. Pre-Mosaic Israelites[135] were naturalists and polytheists. So, very likely, Enoch venerated Nature in the way the Essenes did, and in that way served as their 'founder.' Either way, Moses revered him, and seems to have passed that observance on to the Essenes in a profound way.

We have already shown how early shamanistic traditions influenced the Essenes. Other traditions come from later teachings of **Zarathustra** (Persian origin, around 1750 B.C.E.), who documented the first *truly* monotheistic religion (**Zoroastrianism**), influencing the **Abrahamic religions** (of which Judaism, Christianity, and Islam are branches).

The **Mesopotamians, Babylonians, and Sumerians** followed polytheistic traditions, based on the natural and cosmic forces. All polytheistic religions are simply interpolations upon earlier Animism and Totemism.[136] Where Animism says that 'God' resides in all things; and Totemism says that since 'God' resides in all things, one can choose a thing, name it, and call it 'God' for the expedited and focused purpose of intimate and personal veneration; Polytheism gives names, titles, personalities, backstories, and dramatic twists of fancy to the forces of nature and the cosmos

102

(i.e. Aphrodite, the Greek goddess of love; Aten, the Egyptian god of the sun; Thor, the Norse god of thunder; etc.).

Where **Egypt** becomes a major factor in the history of the Essene tradition, which, as you will recall, is the forerunner of Roman Christian ethics, is when Moses comes into the picture. Documentation on a historical 'Moses' is not substantiated and is subject to debate. At the very least, there is thought to have been a 'Moses-like' figure who existed around the 13th-c. B.C.E. (for the sake of argument, we'll refer to him by the biblical name of 'Moses'). Theoretically, Moses, as a prince of Egypt, would have received the best formal education, and thus would have been familiar with – and arguably influenced by[137] – the traditions of the Indus Valley Civilization, shamanism, and the rest.

Concurrently, **The Vedas** of Hinduism (1500-1200 B.C.E.) emerged from shamanistic origins. The earliest shaman were known as ṛsis (a.k.a. *Mantradraṣṭa, Rishi*, seers). They are regarded as a combination of patriarch, priest, preceptor, scribe, sage, saint, ascetic, prophet, and hermit (sound familiar?). They claimed to have received the Vedic mantras from the Paramātman (the One Law, which is the ultimate reality; Western civilization refer to this as God). They claim the Vedas are "the very breath of the Paramātman in his form as space."[138]

The Essenes, in this sense, are considered shaman, modeling
themselves after the *Rishi* of the ancient Hindus Valley.

Moses is thought to have received the Torah (the first
five books of the Christian Old Testament) directly from
God, in the style of our *Rishi* of the Hindu Tradition.
(Interestingly, the timelines converge here, as Moses'
receiving of the mysteries from God or Enoch –
depending on who you ask – is believed to have
occurred collaterally with the *Rishi's* of India receiving
the holy Vedas.) Moses abandoned his life of privilege
to live in the wilderness, where, as the Essene tradition
describes it, he communed with the forces of nature
and the cosmos, becoming intimately close with God
and Creation (basically, observing the forces of nature
and the cosmos and intuiting the underlying
intelligence/consciousness at their foundation).

The Buddha (the founder of **Buddhism**, Siddhartha
Gautama) was a wandering ascetic religious teacher,
living in South Asia around 450 B.C.E.[139] The Buddha
owned little property, discarded the sensual for the
spiritual, meditated, and communed with the forces of
nature and the cosmos (again, sound familiar?). He is
said to have obtained *nirvana* (what some might call
'Atman realization,' 'Cosmic Consciousness,' or 'Christ
Consciousness'). Buddhism, while not a religion per
se, is a spiritual experience which focuses on ethics
and a proper way of living. The Essenes, according to
Josephus and Philo, were primarily concerned with
ethical teachings, and not those of a mystical nature.

This influence comes from their founding through Enoch and Moses (both naturalists) and from the teachings of the Buddha, with which they would have come into contact during captivity in Persia and through their affiliations with the Roman trade routes.

The **Essenes** considered Enoch their patriarch and Moses their lawgiver, influenced by the teachings of pre-Vedic traditions via the Indus Valley civilization, Sumeria, Egypt, Mesopotamia, Babylon, and Persia. Under Moses they became a distinctly separate sect of Judaism, considered 'keepers of the faith' under Aaron, the first High Priest of Israel. They were also referred to as 'Aaronites' or 'Zadokites,' serving as the High Priests in Solomon's Temple. They were rewarded with position and privilege (religiously speaking) for remaining faithful to the God of Israel and the *true* (allegorical) *teachings* under Moses after the Levites and other priestly factions (literalists) proved unfaithful (the Levites subsequently were made subject to the Zadokites). The Essenes eventually split from mainstream Judaism due to what they perceived as the 'abominations of Israel.' They settled in areas around the Dead Sea (Qumran), Damascus (The Covenanters), and Egypt (Therapeutae), devoting themselves to the study of ancient wisdom, agricultural methods, and social good.

Influenced by the ethical teachings and spiritual focus of the Essenes, John the Baptist, Jesus, John the Beloved, and even the Apostle Paul forwarded this message to Jews and Gentiles in the Jordan River Valley and beyond. These teachings serve as the ethical basis of Roman Christianity and the beginnings of the Christian Church.

Jesus, the Essene Master, taught compassion, love, and acceptance; he modeled right living, in body, emotions, and mind; he offered inspired words of wisdom and peace, as well as healing and moral instruction to those in his sphere; and he sought the 'kingdom of heaven' – that others would choose to turn away from their materialist pursuits in exchange for spiritual communion with the Heavenly Father, the One Law, the Source of all that is material and immaterial, and with one another – in his lifetime.

appendix iii: the evolution of conventional 'truth'

how one person's word can serve as the basis for a global movement (or 'how humankind creates the schema of reality within their minds')

> Whenever you find yourself on the side of the majority, it is time to pause and reflect.
>
> - Mark Twain

To outline how a claim by one person (founded or unfounded; believed by the claimant fully, partially, or not at all – it makes no difference) can become an irrefutable dogma over time, I present *The Doubling Time Paradox* below.

The Doubling Time (Exponential Growth) of Authoritative Statements

1st Generation: A dogmatic statement or claim is made by one enjoying some degree of authority. The Authority may or may not actually believe or have full confidence in this claim, but it serves a beneficial purpose for the Authority.

[1 person who may or may not actually believe the claim].

2nd Generation: A few close, subject, and/or accountable to the authority embrace the statement or claim as very likely - if not true.

[12 people, influenced by the claimant in some fashion, believe the plausibility of the claim and accept it as very likely true.]

107

3rd Generation: The few become resolute and emphatic in their transmission of this claim, influencing yet others.

[144 people now firmly believe the claim, because some whom they respect and trust emphatically presented the claim as true.]

NOTE: To facilitate a claim 'growing legs,' a few conditions typically apply: the claim (1) was made with authority from a place of authority; (2) seemed reasonable or plausible; and (3) could not easily be debunked.

4th Generation: These 144 others, witnessing the emphatic resoluteness of the few, and possibly accepting the claim as likely or true based on the reputation, power, and/or influence of the original Authority, promote the claim to yet others.

[1,728 people now assume the claim must be true.]

5th Generation: The claim or statement of fact is widely accepted by the many (regardless of proof or even rationale) simply on the basis that it is repeated so often and seemingly accepted by a substantial number of others.

[20,736 people who don't think twice about the certainty of the claim.]

6th Generation: The claim is no longer questioned by anyone, fully accepted as a given, and used as its own basis for yet further claims, acts of kindness or violence, and organizations formed to further the institution established by the claim. This might occur even when no one currently alive recalls the initial claim or, perhaps, who originally made the claim (for certain; now people conjecture and debate over the founder of the claim, whether he really existed, and what he really meant, which causes its own rifts).

[248,832 people who emphatically stand by and defend the claim to all comers.]

7th Generation: Another Authority appropriates the claim, now universally accepted as fact, and subjugates it to satisfy other self-serving purposes. Typically, this is accompanied by fraudulent treatment of the context of the original claim and supplemented with manufactured and fabricated additional supporting 'facts': people, places, and concepts; to further legitimate their proprietorship of the original claim. At this point the expansion rate itself doubles, based on sheer scale of force.

[5,971,968 people consider the claim as irrefutable fact and take offense to anyone who does not, starting a large-scale cult based on the claim, maintained by a clergy, a king, and an army.]

8th Generation: The now reconstituted claim continues its proliferation, but in the new paradigm (because *times they are a'changin'*). And the idea of the original claim has been around so long, that - still - no one objects.

[143,327,232 people proclaim a holy war against others who do not accept the claim as universal truth and the means to everlasting salvation, making them 'infidels' and worthy of death.]

9th Generation: Many convert for fear of losing their life and/or means of living. The State sanctions the religion. Foundations are established in its name. Pamphlets are distributed and rallies held to continue the conversion of the unsaved. Many factions emerge based on various contextual interpretations of the claim.

[3,439,853,568 citizens of the planet affiliate with this, the dominant Faith tradition, if for no other reason than because it's all anyone they know seems to believe.]

This happens not only with regard to historical information, but in societal institutions such as government, science, medicine, marketing, and religion (anything can turn into a religion), as well. It really happens with most everything that mankind has a 'finger' in. Memes such as myths, legends, sayings, societal rumors, office chatter, etc. You name it, this *Doubling-Time Paradox* has probably occurred. Below are a few examples of well-known and largely accepted, though unfounded claims from modern history:

o **Historical Myth:** Medieval scholars believed the Earth to be flat.

Verifiable evidence exists in historical records as far back as ancient Greece (and some say as far back as Sumer) that document not only that the Earth was a spheroid, but its precise shape and size. The 'Flat Earth' theory is believed to have originated during the Protestant Revolution during the 17th c.; the Protestants of the time tried to use interpretation of scripture to debunk the teachings of the Roman

110

Catholic Church. This "Flat-Earth" theory was never mainstreamed.

o **Government Falsification:** The Vietnamese torpedoed our naval ships.

The 'Gulf of Tonkin Incident' reportedly occurring on August 4,1964, was used erroneously by President Lyndon B. Johnson as an excuse to initiate U.S. engagement in the Vietnam War. This falsification and deception was confirmed well after the fact by insiders, and documentation has been declassified which verifies this fraudulent use of military intelligence.

o **Scientific Assumptions:** Scientists understand how everything works (i.e. natural processes such as Quantum Mechanics, Gravity, the Strong and Weak Forces, Macro-Evolutionary Processes, and the transition of substance from inanimate to animate/non-living to living).

At the root of most, if not all, scientific research are foundational assumptions (*a priori*) which are used as the basis of inquiry and experimentation, often resulting in actionable data. These assumptions tend to no longer be researched because, assumed to be fundamental, they consistently produce results. But to arrive at the 'known' laws of physics, you have to, ironically, break all of the laws of physics. Below are a few examples of *a priori* scenarios in modern Science.

- The primary example of this is the 'Big Bang Theory,' also known as 'Cosmic Inflation,' which states that at the initial moment of Creation, **matter emerged from nothing.**[140] So, everything we see in the observable

111

universe and that which is a part of the other 99% of the theorized remainder of the material universe – which astrophysicists say we can't see but is likely there (and it may be infinite) – was theoretically compressed into the space smaller than an atom (or maybe no space at all, so *from nothing*), and then exploded violently, sending cosmic dust and radiation expanding **faster than the speed of light** (the cosmic speed limit), in fractions of a second.

So, before the first 10^{-32} of a second of the universe, the two most fundamental laws of physics are broken, that of 'something from nothing' and the cosmic speed limit. By the end of the first second of Creation, **the expansion came to a sudden and equally inexplicable halt** (yet another broken law of physics).

There is more to the story, but the point is that the rules of physics did not seem to apply to get the universe started, until after the first second or so, then they did. Of course, we can't see back further than the first 380,000 years or so because of the cosmic microwave background, the "afterglow" of the Big Bang (thus *a priori*). So, the first 379,999+ years is really anyone's guess.

- The laws of life and living are fairly well understood, but to get to those laws, you must break the known laws of physics by crossing from inanimate to animate, unconscious to conscious. Then, once that law is broken, known biological laws apply. This means that biological laws are *a priori*.

- Celestial physics – the organization of solar systems, galaxies, and clusters – was thought to be well understood until the 1930s, when Swiss astrophysicist Fritz Zwicky discovered there was not enough mass in galaxies to hold them together. In order to make the math work, mass and energy (known commonly as Dark Matter and Dark Energy) were added to the equation. The observable universe now accounts for 5% of the substance of the universe, with 95% relegated to the combination of 'Dark' forces. Of course, they are called 'Dark' because we can't see them and we have absolutely no idea what they are; they are unknown and very possibly unknowable. This logic is what materialists would call 'The God of the Gaps' (when attributed to religion), meaning that 'there are things we can't figure out, so this idea serves as a placeholder in the meantime.' Celestial physics is *a priori*.

I'm not saying that these theories are *wrong*, just that they are based on unknowns, and are by definition *a priori*. To continue with examples in other areas, the following list is presented:

- **Marketing Spin/ Medical Misinformation:** There is no proof that cigarette smoking causes lung cancer.

A 1953 ad for Camel Cigarettes, after lab studies conducted by the R.J. Reynolds Company indicated to the contrary.

- **Religious Fervor:** 'Three Secrets of Fatima,' a claim of sightings of the Virgin Mary by three children in Portugal in 1917.

  The children reported the sightings. No further substantiation was given. The Church sanctioned the reports *ex post facto*. Many have proliferated the veracity of this claim, using reportedly fulfilled (though cryptically-worded) prophecies as the basis.

- **Social Media Melee:** Certain politicians engage in lude and disgusting acts of child trafficking.

  Prior to recent political elections, foreign governments have been suspected of sanctioning Social Media campaigns to subvert and influence the democratic process. Regardless of the source of the misinformation, thousands of social media users have responded in very vocal and violent ways against targeted politicians for alleged illicit activities.

- **Myth Mantra:** Some people are left-brained and some right-brained.

  Psychomythology of unknown origin which is reinforced even by some psychologists. There is no scientific evidence to support this myth.

- **Legends are Born *and* Made:** Billy the Kid was a sadistic psychopath, a demonic agent of Satan, with the skills of a sharpshooter.

  Billy the Kid (William Bonney) of the American Old West (d. 1841) was a real historical figure, and he was involved in a few notorious conflicts, but he was not the ruthless killer he is portrayed to be in romanticized tales, which began to proliferate almost immediately after his death, by serial novelists (historical fiction).

- **Sayings Saturate:** Don't judge a book by its cover.

  In actuality, the cover is a very efficient way to judge a book, as a rule. Most authors and publishers choose the cover design very painstakingly for that very reason. But we continue to say this cliché as if it were coy wisdom.

- **Societal Rumors:** 9/11 was an inside job.

  Conspiracy Theories are the buzz of the modern media age. Often rooted in conjecture based on circumstantial evidence, and even falsified depictions. These claims can become massively popular movements and even affect political, social, and environmental efforts.

- **Office Chatter:** Nancy and Chuck are seeing each other on the down-low.

  Stand by the water cooler at work for a few minutes and see what pops up. Odds are good that the intel has a smattering of truth (maybe Chuck politely held the door open for Nancy once and they happened to exchange smiling glances, which someone with a creative mind imagined as flirtatious and pointed) - maybe - and a lot of circumstantial creative fluff. But then again, sometimes Nancy and Chuck really are seeing each other on the down-low.

The commonality between the above claims is only that there is/was no verifiable proof, they were based on one person's say-so initially, and that many people came to believe the claim as a result, simply from repeated iteration and the intensity and authority of its delivery. We are impressionable creatures by nature. And we go along with claims like these for all sorts of reasons, even if a part of us doesn't 'buy it.'

All this goes to show is that anything, including the teachings of the Ancients, can be subject to errant or fraudulent proliferation. The moral here is to use your own experience, judgment, and intuition to measure claims which are otherwise beyond your capacity to investigate. *A tree is known by its fruit* (The Buddha and the Apostle Paul would agree).

appendix iv: the scientific correlates of the cosmic forces
material vs. immaterial experience

> The Cosmos is all that is or was or ever will be.
>
> - Carl Sagan

We are intimately familiar with our experience of the natural forces of sun (heat/light), air, water, and earth (minerals and nutrients). These are tangible and measurable. The cosmic forces – those of love, wisdom, power, and joy – are a little harder to pin down. We like to think of these as being distinct from the other forces of nature in their essence. My assertion is that they are not. They have correlates in what Science refers to as the 'Fundamental Interactions': the Strong Force (or Strong Interaction), the Weak Force (or Weak Interaction), Electromagnetism, and Gravity.

There are two modes of experiencing the forces of nature and the cosmos, the material experience (science, objective) and the immaterial experience (qualia, subjective). The material experience manifests itself in the physical and chemical reactions of our Lower Self. The immaterial experience manifests itself as the qualitative sensations we experience in our Higher Self. We might refer to these distinctions, then, as 'Lower Experience' and 'Higher Experience.'

A simple example of this tangential paradigm is our perception of color, such as blue or pink, *et al*. Color does not actually exist in the external world around us.

Light waves enter our optical system. (This is the *objective* reality.) Our brain translates this information into the perception of colors in our mind. (This is the *subjective* reality.) Color is a figment of your imagination, in the most literal sense. Further, your experience of the color cyan, for instance, is likely not identical to most others' experience of the same. Your qualitative perception of color is subjective. This same principle applies to aromas, tastes, aesthetics, timbres, etc.

This duplicity is both a material experience and an immaterial one. Material experience is the *objective* reality of the signals from external sources interacting with your sensory mechanisms. Immaterial experience is your mind's *subjective* manipulation of this data into qualitative perceptions, which are unique to each person.

My assertion is that this same duplicity of experience occurs with the four Cosmic Forces as delineated by the Ancients (Love, Wisdom, Power, and Joy), which Science calls the 'Fundamental Interactions.' We tend to think that these interactions occur only within our physical self (our material self), and that is where our experience of them ends. We fail to consider the effect these forces (or interactions) have on our mental – and by extension, spiritual – Being (our immaterial self).

The Ancients referred to the Cosmic Forces as Love, Wisdom, Power, and Joy. Science refers to its 'Four Fundamental Interactions' as the Strong Force, the Weak Force, Electromagnetism, and Gravity. My assertion is that the 'Fundamental Interactions' known to Science, while being experienced in our physical self in obvious and measurable ways, are also experiential to our immaterial self in previously unidentified and unresearched ways.

The scientific interaction of the **Strong Force** is experienced qualitatively as **Love** in our immaterial self. The Strong Interaction binds together protons and neutrons in the atomic nucleus, is responsible for particle creation in high-energy collisions, and is the strongest known fundamental physical force, but is restricted to components of an atomic nucleus (small scale).

Love is defined as "strong affection for another, arising out of kinship or personal ties; devotion; to hold dear" (all definitions in this section are taken from Merriam-Webster).

Love binds us to others, often without logical explanation. If you can explain *why* you love someone, it's probably not love; it's something else. Conditional love is utilitarian and self-serving. We consider true love to be selfless. This feeling of love is most often associated and most strongly felt with family members with whom we share DNA.[141] For those we love to whom we are not closely related (non-familial ties), there is often some other connection which is sensed in our innermost Being – a vibe, a feeling. We are drawn to them, often without logical explanation. You know this feeling. You've had it. There are people your 'spirit' is drawn toward; and others toward whom you are either neutral, or from whom you are repelled. So, this connection can be biological, spiritual, or both. What we have in common in both scenarios is shared essence, whether DNA or spirit (what we might call 'entanglement').

This binding or drawing close of individuals who share DNA or some other fundamental resonance is the Strong Force's influence on us in the immaterial. It is the strongest of the four forces.

The scientific interaction of the **Weak Force** is experienced qualitatively as **Wisdom** in our immaterial self. The Weak Interaction is responsible for particle decay processes in radioactivity. It is 10^{-5} times the strength (and its influence is much less significant than that) of the Strong Force.

Wisdom is defined as "the ability to discern inner qualities and relationships; good sense; accumulated philosophical or scientific knowledge; prudent course of action."

This expression manifests in our lives as good judgement. *It knows its time and place.* The Weak Force is basically the 'death cycle' of particles in the material realm. It is prudent in its timing. *It knows its time and place.* It is the physical representation of Wisdom in the processes of the universe. Without the influence of the Weak Force on our immaterial self, we would not contemplate the preciousness of life, of living, of others, of time. These are the foundational motivators of Wisdom.

Wisdom (the Weak Force) is necessary but overshadowed by Love (the Strong Force) in the best of us. Sometimes someone we love deserves corrective consequences, but is offered mercy and grace instead, because the power of Love (the Strong Force) is greater than that of Wisdom (the Weak Force). This is the Weak Force's influence on us in the immaterial. It is insignificant when compared to Love (the Strong Force).

The scientific interaction of **Electromagnetism** is experienced qualitatively as **Power** in our immaterial self. Electromagnetism regulates interactions between charged particles. It is about one-hundredth the strength of the Strong Force, extends over infinite distances, but is dominant at the atomic and molecular scales (small scale).

Power is defined as "the ability to act or produce an effect; possession of control, authority, or influence over others; a controlling agent; physical might; a source or means of supplying energy."

Electromagnetism is the fundamental driving force of material interaction on the smallest scales. It gets things done. It motivates the processes of nature and the cosmos. But it is most effective at the smallest scales. It is insignificant when compared to the Strong Force. The Fundamental Interaction of Electromagnetism is manifested as Power in our qualitative experience. Power gives us the drive to make things happen, to initiate actions, to energize others and our environs, to take control, to make changes, and increases our strength of will. Its influence on others can be experienced without restriction, but is most effective when expressed in constructive, productive, unassuming ways. In ways that do not overreach. When we try to impose our power beyond its rightful influence, others tend to 'put us in our place,' do not comply, or reject us entirely.

Power (Electromagnetism), when used in league with the forces of Love (the Strong Force) and Wisdom (the Weak Force), is most effective. This is Electromagnetism's influence on us in the immaterial. It is much less significant than Love, but orders of magnitude more influential than Wisdom.

The scientific interaction of **Gravity** is experienced qualitatively as **Joy** in our immaterial self. Gravity is responsible for interactions which occur because of mass between particles. It is 10^{-39} times the strength of the Strong Force, extends over infinite distances, and is dominant at the macroscopic scale (large scale).

Joy is defined as "well-being; a state of happiness or felicity; bliss; gaiety; delight."

While Gravity occurs when particles amass, drawing them into a symbiotic union, it is most intense with large bodies (such as planets and other celestial objects). It is by far the weakest of the forces, as it can be easily overcome by the others. Gravity is manifested in our material self in a couple of notable ways. It is most powerful when things are brought close together. It is unrestricted in its effect, especially on the largest of scales. So, too, is Joy most powerfully experienced when shared with others ('the more the merrier,' as they say) and can be felt at great distances.

But it shares another defining trait, Gravity affects the rate at which time is experienced, as does Joy. The experience of the passing of time when we are joyful is completely different than when we are not. Likewise, when Gravity is strongest, the effect of time is distorted. This is Gravity's influence on us in the immaterial (Joy). It is the weakest of the forces, far weaker than Love (the Strong Force), Power (Electromagnetism), or Wisdom (the Weak Force). It is the least influential, the least consequential, and the most easily subdued of the four forces in our immaterial experience. Our experience of Joy can be enhanced by or easily overcome by the other cosmic forces of Love, Wisdom, and/or Power. Love can overcome all of the other forces, when present.

These correlates are not poetic or symbolic. My claim is that they are actual manifestations of the Fundamental Interactions as delineated in Science, that they are experiential not only in our *material* self but in our *immaterial* self, and that they influence us in real ways. My hope is that this assertion will be proven scientifically one day, affirming my philosophical estimation. And, if not, I still like the parallels. :)

I think the Apostle Paul put it beautifully. "... the greatest of these is love." (1 Corinthians 13:13)

appendix v: the essenes and scriptural interpretation
allegorical vs. literal traditions

History is strewn thick with evidence that a truth is not hard to kill, but a lie, well told, is immortal.

- Mark Twain

In his first-hand accounts of the Essenes, Philo *plainly* states, "...[the Essenes'] philosophical study takes the form of *allegory*, and in this they emulate the tradition of the past." (Read this paragraph several times, until each component and its context registers in your brain, before proceeding. I stress this statement because 2,000 years of religious dogma took a 'wrong turn' at this critical juncture.)

So, let's connect the dots. The Essenes took an oath to the death to maintain and protect the Law (the Essenes were originally referred to as the Zadokites, the first High Priests of Israel from the time of Solomon's Temple ca. 10th c. B.C.E., holding as sacred the teachings of Moses).

Philo states that the Essene's translation of scripture was "mostly allegory."[142] Merriam-Webster defines 'allegory' as "the expression by means of symbolic fictional figures and actions of truths or generalizations about human existence." So, if the Essenes – who took a solemn vow to the death as "keepers of the Faith, descendants of Aaron, first High Priest of Israel," to maintain and protect the esoteric Law of Moses –

believed the scriptures to be allegorical, then Moses must have, too (and by extension the original Zadokite priests, Enoch, and the Ancients).

Philo goes on to state that the Essenes were interested mainly in the *ethical* part of the traditions, not the symbolism and other-worldly accounts or miracles (Fritsch, 106).[143] They were rational, sober naturalists who deduced the underlying Law which dictates all things, based on their observations of the natural and cosmic forces (as did Moses). Further, these were the ethics and beliefs of Jesus, who was regarded as the Essene Master.

If these claims don't add up in your mind based on what you have been told by institutional authorities – beginning with the designer and fabricator influencing the modern version of the canonized scriptures of the Church of Rome (particularly the New Testament; think of it as a patchwork quilt with added pieces of 'flare'), Eusebius, Bishop of Caesarea (the primary spiritual advisor to Emperor Constantine, ca. 4th century C.E.) – this was with intent. Not to doggedly malign this brilliant scholar. Eusebius considered himself a pious individual with the highest ideals in mind, regarding conversion and right living.

It was his methods and tactics that are in question.

To Eusebius, the ends definitely justified the means. Have you ever done the 'wrong thing' for the 'right reasons'? That's what seems to have happened here. Eusebius wrote in his book *Praeparatio evangelica*

(Book XII, Chapter 31), "... it will be necessary sometimes to use falsehood as a remedy for the benefit of those who require such a mode of treatment." He has been famously and repeatedly criticized by historians, both contemporary and recent, as being "the first thoroughly dishonest historian of antiquity" (Jacob Burkhardt, 19th-c. cultural historian).

It was Eusebius, blaming the Jews for the death of Jesus (Christ), that put a decidedly gentile bias into the scriptures of the New Testament. Several times Jesus is 'quoted' as praising gentiles for their expression of faith and, conversely, as being equally disappointed in that of the Jews (i.e. *Jesus Heals a Centurion's Servant*, Matthew 8:5-13).

In 331 C.E., a few short years after the Council of Nicea met to resolve theological disputes in May of 325 C.E., Eusebius was commissioned by Constantine to produce the first series of actual "portable, bound sacred scriptures" (a set of 50 'Bibles' in Greek) for the Bishop of Constantinople and his rapidly expanding congregation).

In the preparation for this monumental undertaking, Eusebius was in position to influence canonized scripture (which was still largely unsettled and ongoing) for his own 'pious' purposes. Eusebius, a master wordsmith, aligns 'facts' of Jesus' life with ancient Hebrew prophecies (Have you ever wondered why the scriptures frequently pointedly proclaim that certain aspects of and occurrences in Jesus's life were *specifically* to 'fulfill scripture' or 'prophecies'?[144] The proverbial 'arrow' is a bit 'on the nose.'), assigned Paul's name to various anonymous and agreeable texts to form the Epistles, adds the Passion story to the original text of 'The Gospel According to John' to align more closely with the Synoptic Gospels (which questionably omit the story of the raising of Lazarus among the count of Jesus' miracles), and co-mingled pagan and non-ecclesiastical concepts into the Jesus narrative to make it more easily absorbed into Roman and Mediterranean sensibilities and traditions. Then copied and bound this construction into the world's first set of 'Bibles.' All substantiated on his authority as the 'Father of Church History,' (as he was then and remains known, due to his vast knowledge), and his exceeding favor with Constantine.

Again, for all the 'right reasons.'

According to his own words, (and allusions which were either expressed or implied) to point the world toward Jesus, the Christ.

To be fair – the Bible hadn't reached its modern accepted form – Eusebius (overseeing prolific libraries as collected by Origen and Pamphilus before him) had access to many and varied versions of scriptural traditions. His 'treatments' amidst the continual process of canonization would hardly have been noticed, given that there was no standardized version of the scriptures at the time, and that he was considered the final authority on all things 'church history.' Every church center had its own version of scripture, even including books of their own choosing.

The form of publication that Constantine commissioned from Eusebius for the Bishop of Constantinople – a portable, bound bible – caught on wildly. The 'cast' had been set; Eusebius had made an indelible mark on canonization through the newly-formatted scriptures into 'Bible' form, to include Eusebius' innovation of separating scripture into units, such as chapters and verses for easy reference. Bibles became the popular medium for the 'Christian-on-the-go' and Eusebius had a template already published. It was just a matter of time and trade before this glorified, gentile-friendly, Pauline-oriented, romanticized (meant in its literal and historical usage) document became the new face of Christianity.

Sources for this section:

Edward Gibbon, "Eusebius of Caesarea: Praeparatio Evangelica,"(trans. E. H. Gifford), Tertullian.org, https://www.tertullian.org/fathers/eusebius_pe_12_book12.htm (retrieved May 17, 2024).

-----, *History of the Decline and Fall of the Roman Empire*, Vol II, Chapter XVI.

Eusebius, *The Life of the Blessed Emperor Constantine, Bk. 4, Ch. 36.*

-----, *Vita Constantini*, IV, 36-37.

Gregory, Caspar Rene (1900). *Textkkritik des Neuen Testaments*. Vol. 1. Leipzig, 22.

Lysander Spooner, *The Deists Reply to the Alleged Supernatural Evidences of Christianity* (Boston: 1896; reprinted by Legare Street Press: 2023), 35-36.

McDonald & Sanders, *The Canon* Debate: 414-415.

R.W. Burgess and Witold Witakowski, *Studies in Eusebian and Post-Eusebian chronography* 1 (Historia, Wiesbaden, Germany, 1999): 69.

Scrivener, *et al.*, *A Plain Introduction to the Criticism of the New Testament* vol. 1 (London: George Bill & Sons): 118-119.

Socrates Scholasticus, *Church History*, Book 1, Chater 1.

Wilson Walker, *A History of the Christian Church* (Scribner, 1958): 108.

notes & bibliography

[1] The reader will also notice plenty of 'notes' throughout this book. While it is a 'guided meditation' (ultimately), some of its claims will cause pause – at the very least – if not a furrowing of the brow, because its tenets seem at the surface to be contrary to modern religious doctrines, which are *based* on the practices presented herein, but which have obscured these teachings and turned them into 'Frankenstein's monster,' if you will. Many of us take religious dogma for granted, as if institutional precepts have always been accepted as irrefutable. This is certainly not the case, for any religious tradition. Many 'hands' have been involved when it comes to the formation of any organized faith system. And many motives, influences, and 'authorities.' This alone creates the opportunity for information to become tainted and/or exaggerated – at the least – or completely fictionalized – at the most – over time.

When you become so accustomed to a misconception that you accept it as the 'God's honest truth,' the actual truth (if and when you are finally presented with it) can shock your sensibilities and make you ask lots of questions – which I did, and have, and continue to do. As I state in this book, "...there are no answers, there are only questions."

This book does serve the purpose of presenting a prescription for a form of 'guided meditation,' but it also makes a foundational argument which requires some consideration before that prescription can (1) make sense, (2) find a welcome home in your Being, and (3) yield 'fruit.'

So you are forewarned, much of the evidence and logic supporting the 'argument' portion of this document can be found here in the 'notes & bibliography' as well as in the appendices. This serves two purposes, which are flip sides of the same coin: (1) The casual reader who does not require much investigative reporting can breeze through the book without wading through pages of supportive documentation and reasoning, and (2) the

130

cynical ('prove-it-to-me') reader has access to an ample resource of citations and notes from which to reference and cross-reference, being presented with the logical basis of each assertion.

[2] The out-of-body experience certainly got my attention and began the process of more diligently seeking answers to my existential questions, but these questions have been with me since I can remember. At the age of eight or so, I can clearly recall sitting with my parents on Sunday mornings at the First Wesleyan Church of Bartlesville, Oklahoma pondering the nature of God. This pondering was a response to the things that Pastor Franklin Hauser had claimed about God: that he was omnipresent, omniscient, omnipotent; that he had no beginning and no end; that he created all things; that we could not fully know his true nature nor his breadth and depth. Asking my dad how God could live forever, his thoughtful explanation to me was that God's lifespan is so immense as compared to ours that it might as well be forever, sort of like a mayfly asking how long we will live. We might as well say 'forever.' Even at that young age, I thought a lot about these concepts, trying to reconcile in my mind something comparable which would make sense of this thing called 'God.'

My first thought was that the nature of God must be energy, because I knew from science class that everything was made of energy, that it could not be lost, that it transferred into and out of forms of matter, and that it was ever present. I soon decided that the nature of God was more like information, which motivated and directed the energy (and all physical processes). I knew that there had to be something immaterial underlying the processes of nature because the physical is finite, and I knew energy was a physical manifestation. This curiosity recaptured my attention following the car accident, more than a decade later, evolving and refining itself as I searched for answers, putting the many disjunct pieces of the puzzle together over time.

[3] Elizabeth Blackburn, Elissa Epel, *The Telomere Effect* (New York: Grand Central Publishing, 2017), 7.

[4] I know, the phrase 'natural and cosmic forces' makes some uneasy, but these are not references to witchcraft nor sorcery (nor *Star Wars*). Hopefully the reader is at least somewhat familiar with the most basic of these forces, which are listed in the reference.

[5] Spoiler Alert: The basic idea of the film *The Truman Show* (Paramount Pictures 1998), is that Truman (the main character) is born into the imaginary world of a TV show, of which he is the star, and of which he is also completely unaware. His entire life is a ruse, scripted by writers and supported by a host of actors who interact with Truman, keeping him on the 'straight and narrow.' The production includes product placements and mini-testimonials of brand-name items, as well as generated weather and lighting effects. Everyone is in on it but him. Until one day, at long last, a lighting canister falls from high above the domed set onto the street below, starting Truman's quest for answers. Yeah, I feel like Truman in this scenario. My 'lighting canister' was the near-death experience, after which I began seeing the 'ropes' behind the 'curtains' in ever-increasing frequency and depth.

[6] Based on L. Frank Baum's *The Wonderful Wizard of Oz* (1900), Metro-Goldwyn-Mayer (1925).

Spoiler Alert: Dorothy, a Kansas farm girl, is swept off via tornado to a fantastic land of witches and wizards; flying monkeys; talking lions, tin men, and scarecrows. She desperately wants to return home, so, with the help of the lion, tin man, and scarecrow, sets out toward the city of Oz to ask the great Wizard how to get home. She eventually discovers that the ruby slippers she's been wearing since landing atop the Wicked Witch of the West near the beginning of the film, are her means to going home. Clicking her heals three times and chanting, "There's no place like home," sends her back home. The irony is that her goal of returning home was always within her means. She just didn't know it.

[7] I. Cross, E. Zubrow, F. Covan, "Musical behaviours and the archaeological record: a preliminary study," *Experimental Archaeology* Vol. 1035 (2002): 25-34.

[8] Muhammed Furkan Gunes, "Ancient site older than Gobeklitepe unearthed in Turkey," Anadolu Ajansi, https://www.aa.com.tr/en/culture/ancient-site-older-than-gobeklitepe-unearthed-in-turkey/1664156#, (retrieved on May 11, 2024).

[9] C. Dougherty, L. Mellor, & S. Jian, *The relationship between Advanced Placement and college graduation*, (National Center for Educational Achievement, 2006).

[10] Ashley A. Smith, "Progress on Remediation," Inside Higher Ed, https://www.insidehighered.com/news/ 2016/01/22/new-complete-college-america-data-remediationshowprogress#:~: text=Each%20year%2C%201.7%20million%20students%20ente ring%20college %20college%20require,and%2045%20percent %20of%20Hispanic%20students%20need%20remediation (retrieved May 14, 2024).

[11] Original document not shown here due to length. Online search: 8th Grade Final Exam, Smoking Valley Genealogical Society and Library, Salina, Kansas. C. 1900.

The document lists questions in areas such as Grammar (i.e. "Give nine rules for the use of capital letters."), Arithmetic (i.e. "Name and define the Fundamental Rules of Arithmetic."), U.S. History (i.e. "Give the epochs into which U.S. History is divided."), Orthography (i.e. "What is meant by the following: alphabet, phonetic, orthography, etymology, syllabication?"), and Geography (i.e. "What is climate? Upon what does climate depend?").

This exam was broken into five timed subsections consisting of a total of forty-eight questions. The entire length of the exam was five hours. Source: Dave Reed, "8th Grade Final Exam, circa 1900," https://davereed.tumblr.com/post/571391973/8th-grade-final-exam-circa-1900 (retrieved on May 11, 2024).

Note: There are several similar exams posted online by various sites, all of which are dated to around this time, and all of which show a standard of knowledge which would stump many (if not most) undergraduate college students today.

[12] The phrase 'empty vessels' in this context refers to the subject's openness and receptivity to new knowledge, understanding, and perspective, as opposed to one who thinks and feels that they know all they need to know and are not open to new possibilities nor perspectives. This concept – originally attributed to Zen Buddhism – passing through many faith traditions, was brought into popular consciousness more recently in James Cameron's *Avatar* (2009), in which the Na'vi character Mo'at states, "It is hard to fill a cup which is already full."

[13] A great place to start reading about the scientific correlate of this ancient philosophy, which I discovered only after concluding my research for this book, is Dr. Elizabeth Blackburn and Dr. Elissa Epel's game-changing research on telomeres, as described beautifully in their book *The Telomere Effect*. I find it inspiring that the teachings of the Ancients align so seamlessly with modern scientific discovery.

This book, *Just Peace,* is based on philosophical principles, many of which find an ally in the sciences. However, I believe the intuition of the Ancients still has much to say that science has yet to resolve.

[14] To be clear, the author is not claiming that ancient peoples did not believe there to be pantheons, deities of various sorts, and other such other-worldly entities. The claim is that the *founders themselves* (the Ancients as distinguished in this text), the enlightened, and those of higher personal evolution and understanding *did not* take the allegorical expressions as literal. This premise is drawn from first-hand accounts of the historic

tradition of interpretation of scripture by the Essenes, who were the 'keepers of the faith' and who sacredly passed the teachings of the Ancients – in their original context – forward in time from one generation to the next. This argument will be established and supported throughout this book.

The thread of commonality itself, originating in the symbols for sun, air, water, and earth found in early graphic representations in reverential displays, winding through the various peace/spiritual traditions of history (from the earliest expressions of animism, totemism, and naturalism; polytheism and angelology; the rise of deism; and eventually to monotheism) demonstrates the origin and development of these teachings over time, dating back to at least the late Pleistocene era (ending approximately 11,700 years ago). The use of names and titles of the forces of nature, of their personification as 'angels' and other deities, was a psychological tool which yielded physiological results.

[15] Philo of Alexandria, *Quod Omnis Probus Liber Sit*, (treatise) OR Philo, as trans. by F. H. Colson in the 10-vol. *Loeb Classical Library* ed., IX, 53-63.

Philo's account of the teachings of the Essenes shows a clear first-hand observation of the nature of their interpretation of scripture as *allegorical*. The Essenes, who were deeply invested in the study of all ancient knowledge, including Sumerian, Mesopotamian, Babylonian, Zoroastrian, Indian, and Oriental traditions, represented the culmination of all ancient teachings, and considered themselves the 'keepers of the Faith,' carriers of the true interpretation of ancient scriptures. If they held as sacred their allegorical interpretations of ancient scriptures from all known written traditions and had passed down this method of interpretation from generation to generation for (some say) thousands upon thousands of years, this would be for a 'posteritous' (my word; meaning 'for the purposes of posterity') reason.

The Essenes did not take their charge to forward Truth lightly. This was a monastic sect whose members each took an oath to the death to preserve these teachings in their original context, as taught to them by Moses (the Lawgiver). This oath was the basis of their acceptance into the sect of the Essenes. Ancient historical documents written by Philo, Plinius, and Josephus describe the agonizing deaths some Essenes endured under the Romans and others while holding fast to this Truth, in no single instance betraying their charge.

This book maintains that the Essenes, 'keepers of the true Faith' since the time of Moses and before, holding fast to this Truth even unto death, famous for their scholarship and rigor in the pursuit of all ancient knowledge (as witnessed by the Dead Sea Scrolls), accumulated and maintained the highest, purest, and most authentic teachings of the Ancients before them in the spirit and context of which they were intended. They guarded and maintained this perspective on ancient teachings jealously because the literal interpretation of 'miracles' and mysticism which had run rampant among sanctioned religious doctrines, and misused for the purposes of power and manipulation by the religious authorities throughout history, had become the dominant and unreproachable interpretation of scripture, according to church authorities, who yielded it on the edge of a sword and with the societal weight of public opinion and scorn.

See 'appendix iii: the evolution of conventional 'truth'' for an explanation and examples of The Doubling Time Paradox.

[16] John 16:12-13.

[17] Surah Al-Ma'idah (5:101).

[18] Kalama Sutta of the Buddha (AN 3:66).

[19] Philippians 4:8, "Finally, beloved, whatever is true, whatever is honorable, whatever is just, whatever is pure, whatever is pleasing, whatever is commendable, if there is any excellence

and if there is anything worthy of praise, think about these things."

These two documented statements from seemingly polar opposite traditions, separated by over four thousand miles and six centuries, express the exact same sentiment. If I were going to paraphrase the Buddha for a Mediterranean audience, I might imagine I would have worded it exactly as Paul did. And this is just one prime example of the wealth of crossover between the peace traditions, or as I like to call it, the 'Thread' (for more information on this 'Thread' see 'appendix ii: the thread.')

[20] The full quote is: "When the student is ready the teacher will appear. When the student is truly ready the teacher will disappear." Often accredited to Lao Tzu without documented basis, this saying has been credited generally to Buddhism, specifically to Zen Buddhism. The Buddhist blogger Bodhipaksa claims that the quote stems from the 1885 book *Light on the Path* by Mabel Collins (1851-1927), though with slightly different wording: "For when the disciple is ready the Master is ready also."

From the website *Tao Te Ching: The Taoism of Lao Tzu*, https://www.taoistic.com/fake-laotzu-quotes/fake-laotzu-quote-When_the_student_is_ ready_the_teacher_will_appear.htm (retrieved May 11, 2024).

[21] Matthew 11:15.

[22] Jean-Pierre Bocquet-Appel, "When the World's Population Took Off: The Springboard of the Neolithic Demographic Transition," *Science* 333 [6042] (July 29, 2011): 560-561.

[23] M. Aubert, A. Brumm, M. Ramli, *et al.* "Pleistocene cave art from Sulawesi, Indonesia," *Nature* 514 (2014): 223-227.

[24] Jimmy Joe, "Shamash: The Ancient Mesopotamian Sun God of Justice and Morality," Timeless Myth,

https://www.timelessmyths.com/mythology/shamash/#:~:text=Sh
amash%2C%20Sin%20and%20Ishtar%20were%20regarded%2
0as%20a,the%20moon%2C%20and%20Ishtar%20denoted%20t
he%20morning%20star (retrieved May 23, 2024).

[25] Britannica, The Editors of Encyclopaedia, "Nature Worship,"
Encyclopedia Britannica, May 25, 2023,
https://www.britannica.com/topic/nature-worship (retrieved May
15, 2024).

[26] Tarapada Bhattacharyya, "The Avesta, Rgveda and Brahma
Cult," *Annals of the Bhandarkar Oriental Research Institute*, vol.
51, no. 1/4 (1970), as a pdf, 31–50, JSTOR,
http://www.jstor.org/stable/41688672 (retrieved May 15, 2024).
[27] J.M. Koller, *Asian* Philosophies, 7th ed. (New York: Prentice
Hall, 2007).

Note: I started to list page numbers that correspond to this reference, but there
are so many, and the book largely address many of the teachings of the Ancients
leading up to the Essenes, that I'm going to just reference the book in general.

[28] Pujyasri Candrasekharendra Srasvati Svami, *Hindu* Dharma
(Bhartiya Vidya Bhavan, 2015), 54-57, 81-94.

[29] A. Bhattacharya, *Hindu Dharma: Introduction to Scriptures and*
Theology (Oxford University Press, 2006), 57-90.

[30] Vivekananda Foundation, *Living at the Source: Yoga
Teachings of Vivekananda*, (Shambhala Dragon Editions, 2001).

Note: This source details many concepts which are aligned with the teachings of
the Ancients, specifically the Essenes. Individual page listings would be tedious
for both the author and the reader. For that reason, the book is referenced as a
whole. The specific concepts in this book which are in common with the other
Peace traditions are expressed in the text as they apply.

[31] The Pluralism Project, "The Dharma: The Teachings of the
Buddha," Harvard University,

https://hwpi.harvard.edu/files/pluralism/files/the_dharma-
the_teachings_of_the_buddha_1.pdf (retrieved May 16, 2024).

[32] Bhikkhu Khantipalo, *The Wheel of Birth and Death* (Buddhist
Publication Society, 1995).

[33] The Ten Commandments, Exodus 20:2-17 (pertaining to ethics
and veneration).

The Essenes taught that God's original Law given to Moses was
singular, 'Love the Lord your God and [by extension] love your
neighbor as yourself' (the "Great Commandment"). If you follow
this law strictly, no other laws are necessary. Moses delivers the
Ten Commandments to the Israelites because they couldn't
faithfully observe the dichotomous one, quibbling over its
splintered applications. The *Torah* was created to speak
specifically to all manner of observations (like, 'If I can't kill, does
that mean anything or just humans, because I enjoy a good
steak now and then'). The *Torah* was not specific enough,
apparently, so the *Talmud* was produced, detailing every
possible interaction in a Jew's daily life.

The Essenes kept it relatively simple, as Law goes, of course
instituting organizational rules and regulations, but not so much
about the minutia of daily life. The Essenes thought of their code
more as 'observances' which were up to the individual to revere
than 'laws' which required punitive measures, with a few
exceptions that dealt directly with the 'love your neighbor' part of
the Law for the sake of community. Infractions of this nature, if
severe enough, could result in expulsion of the individual. For
more information, see the writings of Josephus and Philo.

[34] J.M. Koller, *Asian* Philosophies.

[35] Philip R. Davies, "Dead Sea Scrolls," Encyclopedia Britannica,
May 9, 2024, https://www.britannica.com/topic/Dead-Sea-Scrolls
(retrieved May 15, 2024).

36 Charles T. Fritsch, *The Qumran Community: Its History and Scrolls* (Kessinger's Legacy Reprints, The MacMillan Company, 1956): 111-127.

37 Historical Reference - Genesis 5:21-24 of the Christian Old Testament.

In affiliation with the Essenes, given they considered themselves the 'keepers of the Faith,' the carriers of the Truth as taught by Moses, who – as documented in the Rabbinic kabbalah, via the apocryphal *Book of Jubilees* – was taught by Enoch in his posthumous role as Metatron (the angel of God's word), according to the apocryphal books of *Enoch*. It is in this way that the Essenes considered Enoch to be the founder (or patriarch) of their sect. They were taught and trained in the esoteric teachings of Enoch via Moses and were devout under his brother Aaron, the first High Priest of Israel.

38 F. F. Bruce, *Second Thoughts on the Dead Sea Scrolls* (Paternoster Press, 1956), 101.

The Essenes were followers of the teachings of Moses and served under Moses' brother Aaron, who was the first High Priest of Israel. At this time, the Essenes were referred to as 'Aaronites,' 'Sons of Aaron,' Kohen, '*kohanim*' (meaning "family of priests"), Zadokites, 'Sons of Zadok' (the first high priest in Solomon's Temple) [Exodus 28, 29, 30; Leviticus 21; Numbers 6:23-26, ch.18, 20:22-29; 1 Samuel 2:35; 1 Chronicles 23:13; Ezekiel 43:19, 27, chapters 44:15-31, 48:10-12; Qumran: 4QpIsJM].

39 Charles T. Fritsch, 112-127.

40 Matthew 5: 3-12.

41 Pliny, from his work entitled *Natural History*, claims that the Essenes have existed "through thousands of ages," implying that this order of monks have been vowed to endure the Truth of the

one true 'God' – the One Law - since before history was recorded.

[42] Philo.

[43] Josephus from his work *Wars of the Jews*, II, viii.

[44] *ibid.*

[45] Charles T. Fritsch, 23.

[46] Helmer Ringgren, *The Faith of Qumran: Theology of the Dead Sea Scrolls*, trans. Sander, Emilie T., ed. Charlesworth (James H. Christian Origins Library, Crossroad, New York, 1995), x-xi.

[47] Given that this manuscript fundamentally objects to the idea of the 'supernatural,' the term 'immaterial' is a more appropriate alternative. Something can be *immaterial* and not be *supernatural*. Just because something *immaterial* is not experienced as a part of someone's everyday life does not make it *supernatural* (a.k.a. mystical). All things are natural, meaning 'a product of' or 'consubstantial with' nature. To the Essenes, the One Law is *immaterial* but it/he is not *supernatural*. The 'angels' of the Cosmic Forces are *immaterial* but not beyond experience. Neither of these concepts is beyond or outside of Nature.

The *supernatural* or *mystical* is a fictitious and misguided idea, according to the teachings of the Ancients. The One Law is the originator of all things material and immaterial. He/it is the basis of all that exists. He/it is the most natural thing in the Universe. Not supernatural. Natural. Our material experience is an extension of the fundamental reality.

God is not supernatural. He is Nature itself; meaning that he is all that 'IS,' and within him we reside, as does everything that exists. In Acts 17:28 of the Christian New Testament, it reads, "In Him we live, move, and have our Being." This scripture is based in Essene existential philosophy.

141

48 Helmer Ringgren, xxi.

49 Britta K. Hölzel, Sara W. Lazar, Tim Gard, Zev Schuman-Olivier, David R. Vago, Ulrich Ott "How Does Mindfulness Meditation Work? Proposing Mechanisms of Action from a Conceptual and Neural Perspective," *Perspectives on Psychological Science: A Journal of the Association for Psychological Science* 6 (November 2011).

50 Paul Eslinger, Silke Anders, Tommaso Ballarini, *et al.* "The neuroscience of social feelings: mechanisms of adaptive social functioning," *Neurosci Biobehav Rev.* 128 (2021 Sep): 592-620.

51 N. I. Eisenberger, S. E. Taylor, S. L. Gable, C.J. Hilmert, M.D. Lieberman, "Neural pathways link social support to attenuated neuroendocrine stress responses," *Neuroimage* 35 (2007):1601-1612, National Library of Medicine National Center for Biotechnology Information, https://www.ncbi.nlm.nih.gov/pcm/articles/ PMC8388127/ (retrieved May 12, 2024).

52 Dan Falk, "Is Consciousness Part of the Fabric of the Universe? A theory called panpsychism proposes that consciousness is a fundamental aspect of reality," Scientific American (September 25, 2023), https://www.scientificamerican.com/article/is-consciousness-part-of-the-fabric-of-the-universe1/ (retrieved May 12, 2024).

53 Deuteronomy 31:9.

54 Ernan McMullin, "The Origins of the Field Concept in Physics," *Phys. Perspect.* 4 (2002): 13-39.

55 Steven Weinberg, *Dreams of a Final Theory: The Search for the Fundamental Laws of Nature* (London: Hutchinson Radius, 1993), 211.

[56] Steven Weinberg, *Dreams of a Final Theory: The Search for the Fundamental Laws of Nature.*

[57] Mohammad Reza Pahlavani ed., *Selected Topics in Applications of Quantum* Mechanics (Intech, 2015), 11 (DOI: 10.5772/58514).

[58] Sylvie Braibant, Giorgio Giacomelli, Maurizio Spurio, *Particles and Fundamental Interactions: An Introduction to Particle Physics,* 2nd ed. (Springer 2012).

[59] P. Glansdorff, I. Prigogine, *Thermodynamic Theory of Structure, Stability and Fluctuations* (London Wiley-Interscience: 1971).

[60] From this point forward I will refer to this concept interchangeably as the Source, the One Law, the Creator, the All Father, or Spirit depending on the context. While these labels reference one and the same concept - the underlying creative principle of the universe - they characterize this underlying principle in different manifestations. It is difficult to place the 'supreme being' into a proverbial box.

[61] As examples, the physical processes of nature include thermodynamic processes, mechanical processes, electromagnetic processes, chemical processes, biological process, and geological processes, *et al.*

[62] Douglas. H. Erwin, "The Origin of Bodyplans," *American Zoologist* 39 (3) (1999*)*: 617-629, Integrative and Comparative Biology, https://doi.org/10.1093/icb/39.3.617 (retrieved May 15, 2024).

[63] Eric H. Davidson, Douglas H. Erwin, "Gene regulatory networks and the evolution of animal body plans," *Science,* National Library of Medicine National Center for Biotechnology Information, Science 311 (5762) (Feb 10, 2006):796-800, doi:

10.1126/science.1113832, Science,
https://pubmed.ncbi.nih.gov/16469913/ (retrieved May 12, 2024).

[64] Bruno Hurdy, *et al.*, "Molecular insights into the origin of the
Hox-TALE patterning system," eLife 3:e01939, (2014) doi:
10.7554/eLife.01939,
https://www.nature.com/scitable/blog/accumulating-glitches/the_
evolution_of_body_plans/ (retrieved May 12, 2024).

[65] Peter J. Quesenberry, Sicheng Wen, Laura R. Goldberg, and
Mark S. Dooner, "The universal stem cell," National Library of
Medicine National Center for Biotechnology Information, doi:
10.1038/s41375-022-01715-w,
https://www.ncbi.nlm.nih.gov/pmc/articles/PMC9712109/#:~:text=
These%20observations%20give%20rise%20to%20the%20conce
pt%20of,differentiation%20potential%20as%20it%20progresses
%20through%20cell%20cycle (retrieved May 12, 2024).

[66] Since Hox genes (the genes carrying body plan information)
seem to be universally interchangeable between unrelated
species, the question arises as to where the body plan actually
is. As there is some debate between materialists and
metaphysicians on this subject – with no apparent sufficient and
adequate answer from either side – this issue is decidedly
undecided.

One compelling materialist view is that the body plan does not
actually reside in *just* the Hox gene, but in several accompanying
genes which work together, each contributing to the execution of
the body plan. But even this explanation begs the question(s):
How do any of these 'material' genes 'know' what to do – when,
where, why, and how to successfully execute a body plan? How
do they coordinate? How can they be transplanted into unrelated
biological systems and not 'skip' a proverbial 'beat'?

The implication that a physical system 'knows' a thing, carries
and executes informational processes, can 'make decisions' and
valuative judgments, 'knows' when something is awry, 'knows'

how to repair itself, and 'knows' when to start and stop, makes the deduction seem obvious. Underlying all systems is intelligence. Period.

Intelligence is not within the physical mechanism. It exists in the Abstract (spirit or non-physical realm) and manifests in the physical through processes we do not yet understand. I recognized this concept by the age of nine, though I didn't have the 'tools' of language and scientific understanding that I now have to express these concepts.

[67] Rupert Sheldrake, *Morphic Resonance: The Nature of Formative Causation,* 4th ed. (Park Street Press, 2009).

[68] Helmer Ringgren, *The Faith of Qumran,* 51.

A parallel is drawn here between the essence of the life (or Living) force and that of God (the One Law). In the Essenes' 'War Scroll' (1QM xviii.8), the original scribe states that "(the One Law) acts for the sake of his name," which Ringgren goes on to clarify as meaning that "God does not act because he is affected by man's fate but for his own sake, for the sake of his name or for the sake of his glory." Scriptures in the Christian Bible repeat and reinforce this sentiment (i.e. Ezekiel 36:22). The correlate here is that God "(acting) for the sake of (his) holy name" and the Living Force seeking survival and continuity by whatever means necessary, without regard for particular modes/forms of life (or persons), is analogous.

This presents an intriguing parallel between God and the Living Force. The deduction here is that they are one and the same or at least inseparably interconnected. This also begs the question of references to God as having "breathed life" into man, as recorded in Genesis 2: 7-9 of the Christian Old Testament, as if God and the lifeforce are of the same essence or one in being. According to the Essene esoteric teachings, handed down from Moses, Enoch, and the Ancients before them, this is – in fact – correct.

[69] The question of the 'human experiment' is still under review and could go either way at this point.

[70] Consciousness, Intelligence, and Willfulness in the Cosmic sense:

'Conscious' does not simply mean 'aware,' as is a common perspective. 'Conscious' means to be a part of the ongoing processes of life and the Living Force, because at the root of all that exists – material and immaterial – is consciousness. Even when your brain stops receiving external sensations, every fiber of your being remains active. ('You' are a part of the whole, not separate from it.) We may lose awareness (our ability to perceive, process, and respond to stimulus) for some period of time; say, when we sleep or faint, for instance; but every cell of our body remains 'conscious.' By this definition, physical 'being' never loses 'consciousness' as a function of the Living Force, not even after our 'death,' because, physically, our constituents are recycled into new biological systems below the cellular level.* These constituent parts of what we identify as 'ourselves' continue to be a part of the lifeforce.

Note: It amuses me how we speak of 'losing' or 'gaining' consciousness, or how at some point during the evolutionary process we 'developed' consciousness. This is a materialist frame of reference. From an immaterialist perspective (if you claim to believe in a higher power such as God, by definition you are an immaterialist), consciousness 'becomes' us. Consciousness is ever-present. Matter phases into and out of it, not the other way around.

'Intelligent' in the cosmic sense (of which our local intelligence is like a fractal) does not mean smart, informed, or clever in the way in which we would refer to traits of an intelligent human. Cosmic Intelligence is the ability to navigate and explore an infinite number of possibilities; display an innate relentless curiosity; contain, adapt, and translate all potentialities of form; and express the trait of creativity on a universal scale from the infinitely small to the infinitely large. It (the Source) is also the

146

basis of all mathematical constructs. (The true ones, not the ones that mathematicians dink around with in the attempt to discover the true ones. No offense, mathematicians. We all share in this plight. My philosophic treatise here is my version of "dinking around" with existential constructs. I am certain that my estimations are but triflings to the true nature of the Source.)

'Willfulness' at the cosmic scale manifests itself as the ability to evolve via the unfolding of Cosmic Intelligence. That anything material exists at all, that the matter within our realm self-organizes, interacts with purpose, manifests the Living Force, and is continuously posing 'questions' and pushing boundaries, is the product of willfulness on a cosmic scale.

*See reference: Yongchan Lee, Michael Overholtzer, "After-Death Functions of Cell Death," 92 (4)(Yale J Bio Med, Dec 20 2019): 687-694.

[71] Paul Gilbert, *et al.*, "Learning emotion-focused therapy: The process-experiential approach to change," *American Psychological Association* (Washington, DC US: 2004).

[72] This piece of information is not researched or philosophized. It is anecdotal. This one I know personally. I'm not offering it here as irrefutable evidence to support the thesis portion of this book, just as an explanation as to my sincere and profound interest in this topic. The event described below initiated my deep desire for answers (which we have established are transitory at best).

I vividly recall a near-death, out-of-body experience, which occurred in the early Fall of 1993. My 'consciousness' (awareness) was separated from my body following a violent head-on car collision at highway speed – an accident in which, of the four souls involved, I was the only survivor. I found my 'self' viewing the accident and the surrounding area from a perspective well above my physical body. I surveyed the backed-up traffic, my parents' home in the distance, and the horizon beyond. But I experienced no thoughts, emotions, cares, concerns, attachments, or any of the usual human mental or emotional activities. I no longer identified with my physical, emotional, or mental 'self.' I didn't miss or wonder about my body, mangled in the accident; nor the car, nor my family, nor my friends. I had no valuations nor made any judgments about what had just happened. As a matter of fact, I did not 'think' about the accident at all. Nothing. I was simply aware. Not even just aware; I *was Awareness itself*.

After regaining physical consciousness several minutes later, in my body, in my car, with a medic over me, removing shattered glass from my torso and unbuckling my seatbelt, I felt a sense of confusion (and not the normal kind of confusion associated with experiencing a severe concussion; this was existential confusion). After experiencing total freedom from my body, emotions, and mind... to be back seemed, well, odd. Leaving my material form didn't seem strange to me in the slightest. Returning did.

This near-death experience is what caused me to begin seeking explanations – in religion, in science, in philosophy; anything that might render insight into this, my experience of complete Peace. And to be clear, when I say "Peace" I am not referring to a "peaceful, easy feeling," as the band the Eagles might say. I mean that I did not have *any* cares – for person, place, or thing. None. That is not to say that I felt apathetic. I simply lacked the capacity to feel anything in the way my human form was accustomed. I accepted everything that I observed simply as 'IS' (in the existential sense). And I experienced no negativity toward anything; nor separation from anything.

Peace in the hereafter, according to my experience, is the complete lack of those things that are important to our Lower Self (body, emotions, and the material part of our mind). My 'thoughts' and 'feelings' were no longer proprietary. I 'thought' and 'felt' at the Cosmic level. I accepted all (in the most abstract sense).

[73] My father had a similar experience when he was 21 years old. The doctors told my mother that they "lost him for a time," on the operating table, as the result of a ruptured appendix. My father, some years later, told her that he had an out-of-body experience, and that it was excruciating. He reports viewing the medical staff working to revive him from some height, and hearing screams and wails as if from many suffering souls. These were not the sounds of the people in the operating room or hospital, but from some other unseen source. So, while my experience was pleasant, my father's was not. My father was not a man of many words. He was not prone to exaggeration. And it took years for him to finally divulge this information to my mother.

I discuss the rejection of an impure substance from a living system later in this section. While I have no experience with the concept of reincarnation, if the Abstract acts like a living system (which I propose that it does, because that's what it is), it receives purified souls and rejects impure souls. I imagine that, based on the strong desire of one's Higher Self yearning for communion with the Source, rejection is a rather 'painful' and "excruciating" experience. Something to ponder. Maybe this explains why our Higher Self wants so desperately for us to get our proverbial 'acts together' while in the physical realm.

[74] Yogapedia, "Christ Consciousness," hosted by Yogapedia, https://www.yogapedia.com/definition/5806/ christ-consciousness (retrieved on May 12, 2024).

[75] Ah, you thought Pythagoras just did math. I encourage you to investigate further. His was a rather unusual and interesting sage.

[76] I say "arguably Jesus" because the claim here is that the individuals listed are believed to have experienced 'Christ Consciousness' premortem. But, according to the sequence of events as reported to us in the Christian Gospels of the New Testament, Jesus did not experience 'Cosmic Consciousness' (union with God/the All Father/The One Law/the Abstract) until

after his death (which is when the rest of us experience it – hypothetically). He may have, but there is no documentation confirming that he did. He didn't say he did, and neither does the Christian Bible.

Note: The Apostle Paul referred to Jesus as 'Christ,' but this designation is misunderstood in modern Christianity as a singular event. The concept comes from Hinduism and Buddhism philosophy and is considered attainable by anyone, which is why the Essenes, who were influenced by Buddhist teachings and *from whom* Jesus emerged, so diligently strove to increase their personal evolution. They were each striving to achieve 'Christ Consciousness' and to prepare the way for the Messiah who would bring Christ Consciousness to all (the 'kingdom of heaven'). Jesus' "Good News" was that we each could achieve Higher Consciousness and Commune with the All Father. The idea that Jesus was the *only* human in history who could, did, or would ever achieve sublime status is not good news. It's the opposite. Jesus being "the way, the truth, and the life" simply means that he modeled the Path of Peace and the apex of personal evolution for all humanity. Referencing Jesus' "ascension" as a singular event is a power play that occurred nearly 400 years *ex post facto* by a fascist Church of Rome. It is a control mechanism. But that's a subject for another book.

I include Jesus in this list because, as the master Essene, and as an individual of extremely high ethical and spiritual character, I would rank him with anyone on that list – frankly, at the tippy top. And because of the fact that the term was coined in Western traditions with him in mind.

[77] 1 Corinthians 6:19.

[78] Steven Collins, *Religion and Practical Reason*, eds. Frank Reynold, David Tracy (State Univ of New York Press, 1994), 64.

[79] Qinjing Xiong, Yucui Ju, "Taoism and teaching without words," *Educational Philosophy and Theory* 55 (4) (21 March 2023): 496-507.

[80] About Islam, "This is How Muslims Clean for Prayer," About Islam, https://www.aboutislam.net/spirituality/ this-is-how-muslims-clean-for-prayer (retrieved on May 12, 2024).

[81] Subhamoy Das, "The Hindu Concept of Three Bodies – Body, Mind and Existence," Sanskriti Magazine, https://www.sanskritimagazine.com/hindu-concept-three-bodies-body-mind-existence/ (retrieved on May 12, 2024).

[82] Sandhya Pruthi, *et al.*, "Stress Symptoms: Effects on your body and behavior," Mayo Clinic, https://www.mayoclinic.org/healthy-lifestyles/stress-management/in-depth/stress-symptoms/art-20050987 (retrieved on May 12, 2024).

[83] Eslinger, Paul.

[84] This is paraphrased from a Gandhi quote which was actually, "If we could change ourselves, the tendencies in the world would also change." The paraphrase 'rolls off the tongue' better, certainly.

[85] There are some pretty compelling reincarnation stories published which make one wonder about the potential reality of this concept. Some of the very detailed memories reported from past lives come from very young children raised in Western societies, where reincarnation is not usually considered or discussed. A very interesting online article to read can be found at the reference below.

Lauren Cahn, "Chilling Reincarnation Stories: Meet 6 People Who Lived Before," Reader's Digest, https://www.rd.com/article/chilling-reincarnation-stories/ (retrieved June 1, 2024).

[86] Philo, *Quod Omnis Probus Liber Sit.*

See 'appendix v: the essenes and scriptural interpretation.'

[87] Institute for Quality and Efficiency in Health Care (IQWiG), "In brief: How does the immune system work?" The National Library of Medicine National Center for Biotechnology Information,

https://www.ncbi. nlm.nih.gov/books/NBK279364 (retrieved May 13, 2024).

[88] Jeffrey Curtis Poor, "What Jesus Taught About Most (Hint, It's Not Money)," Rethink: Simple Bible Teachings, https://www.rethinknow.org/what-jesus-taught-about-most-hint-its-not-money/ (retrieved on May 13, 2024).

[89] Matthew 6:9-13.

[90] Sandhya Pruthi, *et al*, "Chronic Stress Puts Your Health at Risk," Mayo Clinic, https://mayoclinic.org/ healthy-lifestyle/stress-management/in-depth/stress/art-20046037 (retrieved on May 13, 2024).

While there are not a lot of studies to be found on the effects of peace on one's health, there are a ton of studies on its opposite: stress. This is one.

[91] It stands to clarify a slight difference in wording which highlights a big difference in concept, that of the terms 'of' and 'with.' 'Peace of mind' refers to a feeling of being safe or protected. It has nothing to do with an actual state of peace. It is based on a feeling, not necessarily an accurate reflection of reality. To say 'Peace with the Mind' refers to the fact that the Mind has a natural order and that we come into alignment with that natural order. This acknowledges that we are subject to universal natural laws and that we are willfully and intentionally bringing ourselves into alignment with this natural order. The same goes for referring to 'Peace with the Emotions' and 'Peace with the Body.'

[92] J.M. Koller, *Asian* Philosophies.

[93] J.M. Koller, *Asian* Philosophies.

[94] Jesus never claims to have healed someone through mystical powers. What he was documented as saying were things like

'stand up/rise up, take your mat/bed and walk/go home'; 'your faith has made you well'; 'stretch out your hand'; 'Go and show yourself to the priest'; with regard to demon possession, he rebukes the demon by saying 'Go'; to the father of a child on their deathbed, 'Go, your son will live'; sometimes he only touched them (sometimes adding spit and mud); or his words were not documented.

[95] To paraphrase, Jesus is saying to the man (and by extension to us all), 'Stop abusing your body, emotions, and mind with wrong thoughts, words, and deeds.' We ourselves are responsible for much (if not most, if not all) of the infirmity within ourselves due to poor lifestyle choices. Buddhists and Hindus would call this level of accountability *karma*.

Encyclopedia Britannica, 11th Edition, Volume 15, New York, pp. 679-680, Article on Karma; Quote – "Karma meaning deed or action; in addition, it also has philosophical and technical meaning, denoting a person's deeds as determining his future lot."

[96] The opposite effect is reported to have occurred in Jesus' own (so-called) hometown of Nazareth, wherein he and his family were known. The Gospels clearly indicate that Jesus "did not do many deeds of power there." Those familiar with Jesus were not 'mystified' by his reputation as a healer nor convinced by his teachings. They did not 'believe' in his powers, and therefore could not (or would not) be healed. In short, they were of "little faith." In both instances, and on both ends of the spectrum, the subject's own faith seems to be the catalyst, a requisite, of healing. (Matthew 13:54-58)

[97] To keep from inundating this section with citations, all information about the lifestyle of the Essenes cited here can be found in the previously cited writings of Josephus, Plinius, and Philo.

[98] Elizabeth Blackburn, Elissa Epel, *The Telomere Effect*, 193-195.

[99] Andew Kovacs, "How Much DNA Do Humans Share With Other Animals and Plants?" The DNA Tests, https://www.thednatests.com/how-much-dna-do-humans-share-with-other-animals/#:~:text=A%3A%20Humans%20share%20a%20small%20percentage%20of%20their,and%20plants%20is%20much%20lower%20compared%20to%20animals (retrieved on May 14, 2024).

[100] Carol DerSarkissian, "What Are Biological Rhythms?" WebMd, https://www.webmd.com/a-to-z-guides/what-are-biological-rhythms (retrieved on May 14, 2024).

[101] Note about the daily routine as prescribed by the Essenes:

Ablutions: this simply means bathing, showering, or washing the body. The Essenes prescribed cold-water ablutions as a means of stimulating the body and mind, awakening very soberly all aspects of one's Being, to include the cardiovascular system and neural processes.

The Garden: The Essenes, having separated themselves from mainstream society, congregating in agricultural cooperatives, literally spent time in the garden with their plants and the elements of the earth, and exposing themselves to sun, water, and fresh air. This is in fact the healthiest scenario, not only for your physical body, but for your emotions and mind, as well. However, there were Ancients (such as John the Baptist, Jesus, and Pythagoras, for example) who had special callings, such as teaching and/or healing, *et al.*, who spent time primarily engaging in what some might call 'missions' work. These individuals were also well versed in working in the literal garden, but cultivated more metaphorical 'gardens,' as well. Following your Calling and/or working a Vocation can be considered your

'Garden' (though I would highly recommend engaging in actual gardening as well, for its healing and peace benefits).

Meals in Silence: The Essenes prepared for their meals with a sense of introspection, by meditating, praying, and feeling a deep sense of gratefulness. Ingesting food is the single most important contribution you make to your health. It plays a critical role in your body's ability to function optimally. And not just the quality and quantity of foods you ingest, but the manner and state in which you ingest them. If you are experiencing stress and anxiety, your body cannot properly digest food - meaning that even the healthiest foods are not fully realized into your system.

Two Meals per Day: You will notice that the Essene daily routine only consists of the noon and evening meals. No place is given for a morning meal. The Essenes integrated sixteen hours of fasting into their daily schedule as a regular practice, abstaining from food between dusk and noon the next day. This fasting allowed the body to process the previous day's meals and regulate the physical systems to their most optimal state. It also served as a method of improving self-discipline and strength of will. While fasting, one is allowed to ingest water and natural fruit juices.

[102] Amy Baldwin, *et al.*, "11.1 Taking Care of Your Physical Health," Open Stax, https://www.openstax.org/books/college-success/pages/11-1-taking-care-of-your-physical-health#:~:text=While%20it's%20not%20the%20only%20thing%20that%20contributes,way%20they%20function%20optimally%20is%20with%20good%20nutrition (retrieved on May 14, 2024).

[103] Robert Kiltz, "The Standard American Diet: What is it and Where do we go Next?" Doctor Kiltz, https://www.doctorkiltz.com/standard-american-diet/ (retrieved on May 14, 2024).

[104] Lisa Wimmer, "Dig into the benefits of gardening," Mayo Clinic Health System, https://www.mayoclinichealthsystem. org/hometown-health/speaking-of-health/dig-into-the-benefits-of-gardening (retrieved on May 14, 2024).

[105] Laurie L. Dove, "Does food packaging affect its nutritional value?" How Stuff Works, https://www.recipes.howstuffworks. com/food-packaging-affect-nutritional-value.htm (retrieved on May 14, 2024).

[106] Krish Tangella, "Does Freezing My Food Affect Its Nutritional Content," DoveMed, https://www.dovemed .com/healthy-living/wellness-center/does-freezing-my-food-affect-its-nutritional-content (retrieved on May 13, 2024).

[107] Becky Bell, ed. Sarah Matysiak, "How Cooking Affects the Nutrient Content of Foods," healthline, https://www.healthline.co m/nutrition/raw-food-vs-cooked-food#TOC_TITLE_HDR_9 (retrieved on May 14, 2024).

[108] M. Buiatti, *et al.*, "The application of GMOs in agriculture and in food production for a better nutrition: two different scientific viewpoints," National Library of Medicine National Center for Biotechnology Information,https://www.ncbi.nlm.nih.gov/pmc /articles/PMC3639326/#:~:text=Many%20concerns%20have%20 been%20raised%20for%20the%20environment%3A,increase%2 0in%20the%20use%20of%20chemicals%20in%20agriculture (retrieved on May 14, 2024).

Note: The intent of this 'paper' is not to disparage GMOs in agriculture and food production. It simply poses two opposing viewpoints. While there are many proposed benefits as well as adverse consequences of GMOs, and many hopes and concerns for the future of this mode of food production expressed in various media, we won't have a clear verdict on the long-term benefits and/or detriments on the health of humans and the environment for some time to come. My personal intuition tells me that any modification of the genome is dangerous and will likely result in potentially catastrophic health consequences for both ourselves and the ecology of the planet.

[109] Elizabeth Blackburn, Elissa Epel, *The Telomere Effect*, 237.

[110] Evelyne Battaglia Richi, *et al.* "Health Risks Associated with Meat Consumption: A Review of Epidemiological Studies," National Library of Medicine National Center for Biotechnology Information. https://www.pubmed.ncbi.nlm.nih.gov/26780279 /#:~:text=Recent%20evidence%20from%20large%20prospective %20US%20and%20European,type%202%20diabetes%2C%20i n%20both%20men%20and%20women(retrieved on May 14, 2024).

[111] National Geographic, "Eating meat has 'dire' consequences for the planet, says report," National Geographic, https://www.nationalgeographic.com/environment/article/commis sion-report-great-food-transformation-plant-diet-climate-change (retrieved May 14, 2024).

[112] The Essenes at Qumran used indoor communal baths for the purpose of ablutions, which they performed up to three times per day. Their attention to hygiene and cleanliness was noted by contemporary historians.

[113] Reid Health, "The connection between stress, busyness, and mental health," https://www.reidhealth .org/blog/the-connection-between-stress-busyness-and-mental-health (retrieved on May 14, 2024).

[114] David DiSalvo, "How Breathing Calms Your Brain, And Other Science-Based Benefits of Controlled Breathing," Forbes, https://www.forbes.com/sites/daviddisalvo/2017/11/29/how-breathing-calms-your-brain-and-other-science-based-benefits-of-controlled-breathing/?sh=307a2dff2221 (retrieved on May 14, 2024).

[115] Melanie Greenberg, "Nine Essential Qualities of Mindfulness," Psychology Today, https://www.psychology today.com/us/blog/the-mindful-self-express/201202/nine-essential-qualities-mindfulness (retrieved on May 14, 2024).

[116] Edmond Bordeaux Szekely, *The Teachings of the Essenes from Enoch to The Dead Sea Scrolls* (U. S. A.: International Biogenic Society 1977).

Szekely, *The Essene Gospel of Peace: The Complete 4 Books in One Volume*, (U. S. A.: AudioEnlightenment: 2018).

Note: It is to Dr. Szekely and his lifetime of scholarship on the Essenes to which I owe a number of the foundational concepts in this book. Not without controversy, Dr. Szekely delivered a message of simplicity, health, and peace to those who adored him and heeded his teachings, shared from the wisdom of the Ancients. He was truly a remarkable man, as represented by his steadfastness and resolve, kindness and humanity, and the legacy which he has left behind. *A tree is known by its fruit.*

[117] See 'appendix iv: the scientific correlates of the cosmic forces' for corollaries between the scientific 'Fundamental Interactions' and the Ancients' 'Cosmic Forces' as proposed by the author.

[118] Edmond Bordeaux Szekely, *The Teaching of the Essenes from Enoch to the Dead Sea Scrolls*.

[119] The reader might interject that Jesus, the so-called Essene Master, did not maintain food and shelter, and had only minimal clothing (at least during his public ministry as recorded in the Bible), as an "A-Ha!" to the Essenes' distinction between frugality and poverty as stated here. While this is true regarding Jesus' ministry, what many are unaware, was that Jesus, as part of the community of Essenes, had shelter and food everywhere he travelled. And that clothing was supplied as needs required. The Essenes are documented to have had numerous satellites around Judea and the extended area. They served as points of trade and philanthropy (social good) for the Community, as well as hosts for Essenes travelling in the course of their missionary activities. The Bible does not document this, but the historians mentioned in this book, such as Josephus and Philo, do.

[120] Dave Ramsey, *Financial Peace: Restoring Financial Hope to You and Your Family* (Viking Penguin, a division of Penguin Press, 1997), 107-123.

[121] The reader might have noticed the repeated use of the term 'deviation(s)' throughout this text. An interesting perspective of the Essenes which is a stark departure from other religious teachings, is the use of the term 'deviation' in the place of 'sin.' While some translations of Essene writings use the word 'sin,' this is not in keeping with Essene philosophy. The Essenes viewed transgressions as a *deviation* from the Path of Peace, which required a course correction; not as a 'sin' which required punishment, shame, penance, or spiritual restitution.

A paired concept is the term 'repent,' which, in its original context, meant "to turn about," or to 'face the other direction,' as translated from the Hebrew word *sheenbeyt* in scripture. Modern dictionaries have amended the official definition to reflect its more-recently-acquired religious nature, to include a feeling of regret and remorse; but this is an adaptation based on popular usage, not on original context. The original concept of repentance was simply to 'change directions.' It was a navigational directive.

The Essenes, in keeping with this perspective, did not advocate shame and guilt for wrongdoings. They simply 'course corrected,' and moved on. This 'take' on the concept of 'repentance' corresponds with their use of the term 'deviation' for wrongful or errant thoughts, words, or deeds. Guilt and shame are not in keeping with the Essene prescription of one's maintaining the highest thoughts, emotions, and actions.

[122] Oliver Gruebner, *et al.*, "Cities and Mental Health," National Library of Medicine National Center for Biotechnology Information,
https://www.ncbi.nlm.nih.gov/pmc/articles/PMC5374256/#:~:text=With%20growing%20urbanization%2C%20more%20and%20more%20people%20are,better%20access%20to%20health%20care

%2C%20employment%2C%20and%20education (retrieved May 14, 2024).

123 Elizabeth Blackburn, Elissa Epel, *The Telomere Effect*, 255-275.

124 *ibid.*

125 Patricia A. Thomas, "Family Relationships and Well-Being," National Library of Medicine National Center for Biotechnology Information, https://www.ncbi.nlm.nih.gov/pmc/articles/PMC5954612/ (retrieved on May 14, 2024).

126 Sang-Yong Eom, *et al.*, "Health effects of environmental pollution in population living near industrial complex areas in Korea," National Library of Medicine National Center for Biotechnology Information, https://www.ncbi.nlm.nih.gov/pmc/articles/PMC5903037/ (retrieved on May 14, 2024).

127 Elizabeth Blackburn, Elissa Epel, *The Telomere Effect*, 255-275.

128 Brandon Gaille, "75 Catchy Washing Machine Slogans," Brandon Gaille Small Business and Marketing Advice, https://www. brandongaille.com/75-catchy-washing-machine-slogans/ (retrieved May 14, 2024).

Note: One early washing machine slogan read "Giving you time back for the important things."

129 A. C. Page, V. Locke, & M. Trio, "An online measure of thought suppression," *Journal of Personality and Social Psychology* 88 (2005): 421-431.

130 Paraphrase of John 1:4.

If a claim is not cited, it is because it has been cited previously.

I use 'shaman' here in both the singular and the plural (my adaptation). I don't care for the plural form 'shamans.' It just doesn't sound right to me. Author's privilege.

Pujyasri Candrasekharendra Srasvati Svami, *Hindu* Dharma, 27.

According to Biblical tradition. This is likely a conflated translation of ancient texts as the original words can be interpreted several ways, one of which is simply that "God moved Enoch from one place to another," or that "Enoch was moved by God," as if to say that Enoch felt divinely-inspired to remove himself to another place, to set himself apart. This 'setting apart' is a common theme among ancient sages, prophets, and shaman, who sought to communion exclusively with the All Father.

You really can't call them 'Israelites' at this time, as Jacob – whose name was changed to *Israel* after wrestling God, or an angel, depending on who you ask (according to scripture; ca. 1906 B.C.E.) – begins that lineage (Enoch lived ca. 3049-2684 B.C.E.), but it serves the purpose of identification.

You might also refer to them as Hebrews (*ivri*, which translates as 'migrant;' interestingly, the plural for *ivri is Ivrim*, also spelled *Ibrim*, which is strikingly similar to the so-called 'Father of the Hebrews,' Abram, later referred to as Abraham), or Jews (Yehudi, derived from the Hebrew name Judah – one of Jacob's twelve sons), neither of which apply during Enoch's time either).

The Christian Bible arguably refers to this Semitic people as "Hebrews" as far back as the time of Noah (Genesis 10:21; in this reference Noah's son Shem is said to be the "father of all the children of Eber," which some argue is the origin of 'Hebrew'; or Genesis 14:13, where the term 'Hebrew' is used explicitly as an identifier with Abram). Considering the former is correct (yielding the benefit of doubt), the 'Hebrews' of Enoch's time still could not be referred to as 'Hebrews' because Noah was Enoch's great grandson through Methuselah, and the scripture reference states that the "children of Eber" were Shem's descendants. This places the term at least four or more generations *after* Enoch.

However, historians do not seem to agree with the biblical timeline of the assigning of the label 'Hebrews' to the descendants of Adam, Enoch, Noah, or Shem. This people are rarely mentioned in non-biblical historical records, because the established 'superpowers' of the time (ranging from Mesopotamia to Rome – or at least Greece), did not account for them. To the dominant civilizations of a few millennia, these nomadic tribal herdsmen were insignificant – politically and militarily speaking.

According to Egyptian records, what mention these tribes do merit is an overarching moniker "Wretched Asiatics" at worst, and 'Semitics' at best. But even *Semitics* (obsolete reference originating from the name of Noah's son 'Shem') does not refer specifically to the 'Hebrews,' as it lumps together a large swath of tribal populations from northwestern Mesopotamia, specifically from the upper courses of the two large-scale rivers in Western Asia, the Tigris and Euphrates, to include Arabs, Jews, Akkadians, the Shashu, and Phoenicians, among others.

Their label aside (and back to the argument referenced here), these Semitic clans were Naturalists and Polytheists before, during, and after Enoch's time (Enoch was an exception, being a naturalist, and not a polytheist) until the time of Moses, according to historical observations. They believed in nature as the source of cosmic wisdom and that every tribe had its own god or gods. Under Abraham they observed Henotheism ("our god is the best"). Moses, after his time in the desert, discovered the One Law and attempted to deliver this message to the Hebrews, with little success. The Essenes were the only ones to adopt this philosophy. Even Aaron, Moses' brother, facilitated the continuation of Henotheism under pressure from the Hebrew masses during the Exodus. Subsequently, the prophets of Israel after Moses' time developed what is known today as a loose form of 'monotheism' (which still really isn't monotheism according to the Council of Nicea in 325 C.E. and further defined at the First Council of Constantinople in 381 C.E.), given you have a three-person godhead, a host of angels and demons, and a satanic figure who rules over the underworld; that's what one calls 'polytheism,' in its purest sense).

So, to clarify and summarize, what we refer to as 'Hebrews' today are referenced by the Romans as 'Jews' by 600 B.C.E. (referencing the 'people of Judah), Hebrews for certain by ca. 1446-1300 B.C.E. under Moses (if he in fact authored the Pentateuch – Genesis, Exodus, Leviticus, Numbers, and Deuteronomy of the Old Testament; there is disagreement as to when 'Moses' lived); and 'Israelites' as far back as ca. 1906 B.C.E. according to scriptural estimations. Prior to this, we have record of their designation as 'Semitics' (a reference to the descendants of Shem), which do not specify Jews as we now refer to them, but group them together with Arabs and others of Northwestern-Mesopotamian origins.

In Enoch's time, this people, now known as the 'Jews,' would have been referred to generally as 'Asiatic migrant tribes,' if at all. Today, the above-referenced labels have been agreed to mean: Hebrews (the culture), Israelites (the race), and Jews (the religion).

Reference: Barbara A. Hanger, "When did the Israelites become known as Hebrews and Jews?" ebible, https://www.ebible.com/questions/8762-when-did-the-israelites-become-known-as-hebrews-and-jews (retrieved on May 25, 2024).

[136] Polytheism was a logical extension of Animism and Totemism. The evolution of 'isms' is summarized here.

163

Animism is the belief that 'spirit imbues all Creation.' **Natural-ism** is very similar to Animism, except that the focus is strictly on nature and the natural processes, as if to say that God is (in) the process of nature, not specifically in any one physical entity, such as a tree or a cow. **Totemism** is the adoption of one particular animal or object to serve as one's personal god, which contains God's spirit. This totem is different for every person and it is up to them what animal or object they choose (this is still true of modern Hinduism.) It doesn't mean that the person thinks their totem is the one and only god. It just means, 'God is in everything and I choose to venerate this 'piece of God' so I can facilitate an intimate experience of relationship with him/it.'

Hinduism, likely the first formal 'religion,' introduced **shaman-ism** as a way of mediating the spirit realm. Then came along **polytheism**, which, as you can see, is basically Totemism on 'steroids,' wherein we add names, titles, personalities, backstory, and human drama to the forces of nature and the cosmos to make them more like us. Creatives of every generation try to embellish upon their deities and sacred rituals. This is not new to humanity nor is it restricted to religious traditions. It's because we are creative and have imaginations.

Monotheism says that God is the supreme ruler of the universe. That all that exists and that everything else is simply a manifestation of God. So we kinda come back around to Animism/Naturalism, except now we look at God as more of a singularity and downplay the sacredness of 'his' manifestations in the material universe. Monotheism considers itself distinct from polytheism but adopts the polytheistic trend of assigning names and titles – even human traits and drama – to spiritual beings (**angelology**). This is terrific irony. This is like saying that the Greek pantheon is monotheistic because Zeus is in charge over all other gods. Greek mythology, I think most would agree, is clearly polytheism.

Henotheism means that there are many gods, but the one for our country/culture/people is "the best" (Israelites approximately from Abraham until Moses). **Buddhism** is the most recent addition of the major 'isms.' It is not a religion, per se. It is a naturalist ethic. It doesn't seem to care as much about the spiritual realm as it does how one behaves and evolves while in this mortal life (the Essenes were influenced by this concept).

Atheism has likely existed throughout time, a natural rejection of the establishment. Atheism says, 'What I know is what I see and that's good enough for me.' **Agnosticism**, also a time-tested companion to spiritual traditions, simply states that 'Yeah, there is a lot going on that I can't know, so I'm good either way.' There are other 'isms' not addressed here, but the above are the major players.

[137] The main argument for Moses being influenced by shamanistic teachings is that he abandoned his princely upbringing and lavish lifestyle to live in the desert for forty years, discarding the teachings of the Egyptian priests for the wisdom of nature.

[138] Pujyasri Candrasekharendra Srasvati Svami, *Hindu* Dharma, 28.

[139] The Buddha was teaching around the same time that the Hebrews were returning to the 'Holy Land' from captivity in Persia. The more informed, such as the priestly classes of the Hebrews – especially the Essenes –would have been familiar with Buddhist teachings and philosophy.

[140] Some say that the term 'nothing' is misleading, and that the compression was simply the smallest possible singularity, which is the definition of a black hole, which means that this initial singularity would have had to radiate at its horizon and poles, ejecting energetic mass via its accretion disk and plasma jets, which means there would have been lots of stuff in the universe prior to the 10^{-32} of a second of the initial act of spontaneous cosmic inflation.

[141] We all have family members with whom we share DNA, who we might say we do not *love*. Love is a complicated and multi-faceted concept. In this case, even with these family members there is a connection which causes us some degree of loyalty or sense of protectiveness. Often, when we say we do not 'love' a certain family member, what we mean is that we do not 'like' that person. There tends to be some degree of deep-seated connection to this person even if we hold some sort of malice or angst toward them. It takes a lot to overcome that connection.

[142] The part of their philosophy that was *not* allegory was their idea that the Source, the One Law, the All Father, God was conscious, intelligent, and willful. All other teachings, such as their use of angelology, were considered allegorical.

[143] One apparent contradiction to the claim that the Essenes "were interested mainly in the ethical part of the traditions, not the symbolism and other-worldly accounts or miracles" is that they were the authors of a substantial amount of eschatological (apocalyptic) writing, as well as highly symbolic and other-worldly literature such as the *Book of Enoch.* Historical context sheds light on this juxtaposition of philosophical ideas.

The Essenes were sympathetic to the *Messianic* movement among Jews of Judea, writing anti-imperialist literature in very flowery and poetic language (which is antithetical because they also believed in the predestination and divine 'appointment' of authority). They were also very well educated and spoke metaphorically of a great many things. Their scribes (writers) were gifted at creating vivid imagery and compelling treatises. As an expression of this creativity, as is witnessed by the evolution of humanity's spiritual traditions over time, an expansion and elaboration of concepts is inevitable. To parse out their true doctrine, as opposed to their social and political commentary, one must look at their *Manual of Discipline*, their lifestyle, and their daily regimen.

[144] Matthew 1:22.

index

167

168

172

173

37, 39, 43, 50, 51, 58, 59,
80, 88, 106, 116, 125, 148,
150, 151, 152, 153, 154
Mind, 1, 3, 5, 11, 13, 25, 28,
30, 80, 151, 152
Mind of God, 25
mindful, 17, 26, 32, 42, 53,
157
mindfulness, 42, 157
Mindfulness, 43, 68, 142,
157
miracles, xi, 125, 127, 136
mobile device, 43
moderation, 15, 41, 87
MODERATION, 41
modern, vii, viii, x, xi, xv, xviii,
4, 38, 41, 94, 110, 115,
125, 127, 130, 134, 150
monotheistic, 102
Morphic Resonance, 7, 145
Moses, xvi, xvii, xviii, 4, 14,
102, 103, 104, 105, 124,
125, 136, 140, 145, 162,
165
Mother Earth, xix, 21
M-Theory, 4
Muhammad, xii, xiii
music, 43
Myan, viii
mysteries, x, xiii, 102, 104
mystical, 61, 104, 152
mysticism, x, 88, 136

Native Americans, ix

natural forces, x, xii, xv, 40,
86
natural fruit juices, 45, 155
natural law, v, xviii, 1, 31
natural phenomena, xi
natural remedies, xvii
natural world, 1
naturalistic, 17
naturalists, 102, 105, 125
nature, v, ix, x, xvii, xviii, 1, 3,
4, 6, 7, 14, 15, 17, 18, 26,
29, 35, 36, 40, 42, 43, 50,
51, 59, 64, 66, 74, 76, 77,
79, 95, 98, 99, 104, 116,
135, 138, 143, 144, 162,
164
Nature, xi, xvii, 2, 7, 8, 14, 21,
29, 30, 31, 44, 55, 56, 60,
61, 63, 65, 68, 69, 71, 72,
74, 77, 78, 79, 83, 84, 102,
137, 138, 142, 145
near-death experience, vii,
132, 148
Neolithic, xv, 99, 100, 137
Neolithic Revolution, xv, 99
neural circuits, 5
neuroses, 41
nirvana, 104
Nirvana, 13
nutritional value, 39, 156

observation, xi, 1, 7, 135
observations, xi, 6, 125
Old Testament, xvi, 104, 140
One Law, 4, 8, 23, 58, 77, 145

175

176

177

179

Made in the USA
Columbia, SC
26 July 2024

38630340R00113